BYTEing Deeper Into Your TIMEX Sinclair 1000

BYTEing Deeper Into Your TIMEX Sinclair 1000

MARK HARRISON

1807 175 YEARS OF PUBLISHING 1982

John Wiley & Sons, Inc.

New York • Chichester • Brisbane • Toronto • Singapore

Library of Congress Cataloging in Publication Data:

Harrison, Mark Richard

Byeting Deeper Into Your Timex Sinclair 1000

82-061778

ISBN 0-471-89888-0

Printed in the United States of America

82 83 10 9 8 7 6 5 4 3 2 1

About the Author

Mark Harrison is a mathematician and computer scientist currently studying at the Royal Holloway College, London University. He has contributed programs to various magazines, including PERSONAL COMPUTER WORLD, a major U.K. publication. The success of this book in the United Kingdom has encouraged Harrison to plan additional computer titles.

Preface

In February 1980 the British electronic pioneer Clive Sinclair introduced a personal computer costing less than $300 which was called the ZX80 and based around the NEC 780–1 microprocessor chip. Apart from being remarkably low in price compared with its American rivals like the Pet, the Apple, etc, the ZX80 had several unique facilities including a "one-touch" keyword entry for commands like RUN, PRINT, INPUT etc, and a syntax check whereby program lines are accepted only if they are syntactically correct. The ZX80 was able to be produced at a relatively low price by using fewer and more powerful silicon chips than had been used previously in similar systems. The one concession made in achieving a low price was to use the microprocessor chip to drive the television display and the cassette interface, in addition to processing data. This was noticeable by the television picture disappearing when information was entered from the keyboard or cassette, or when a calculation was undergone and reappearing when the work had been completed. By November 1980 the ZX80 was outselling all the other personal computers combined in the U.K. market.

The ZX80 was superseded in March 1981 when Sinclair unleashed the ZX81. Although the ZX81 was more powerful than its predecessor, it was built using only four silicon chips and so could be produced and sold for about $200. The ZX81 had overcome the screen flicker of the ZX80 by keeping the display refreshed during the processing of the data and so animated displays were feasible. By replacing one of the silicon chips in the ZX80 it was possible to give it all the facilities of the ZX81 except the animated graphics.

Byteing Deeper into Your TIMEX Sinclair 1000 is designed for both those who have no previous computing experience and others who are not new to computing but require more assistance in operating the ZX81 (or ZX80 with 8K ROM) computer system than the operating manual gives. It starts from the first principles and then, with reference to examples, progresses to some of the most advanced techniques that can be used on the ZX81.

I would like to thank Dr. Graham Beech of Sigma Technical Press for his valuable guidance and encouragement, and G. H. Hogg & Sons Ltd. for use of their equipment.

MARK R. HARRISON

Note to the U.S. Edition

Readers of this book will notice that while the title says it is for the Timex Sinclair 1000, the text refers to the computers as the ZX81. The original ZX81 computer is now being sold exclusively in the United States by Timex Corp. It has been upgraded slightly and is now a 2K Computer. However, all of the programs in this book will run either on your ZX81 or the Timex Sinclair 1000 with no alteration. The techniques of learning BASIC will also be exactly the same on both computers. Whichever model you have, good luck and happy programming.

Contents

Index of Program Listings

BYTEing Deeper Into Your TIMEX Sinclair 1000

CHAPTER ONE

The Principles of a Computer System

Before learning about the capabilities of the ZX81, it is both useful and interesting to understand the basics of a computer system and find out what happens inside a computer when it processes information.

Briefly a *computer*, the main components of which are shown in Figure 1.1, can be described as a digital electronic device which uses a stored list of commands known as a program.

The control, the arithmetic and logic unit, and the memory are electronic circuits. In recent years these circuits have been miniaturized onto chips of silicon only 5 mm square. These microcircuits are called *silicon chips* or *integrated circuits*.

INPUT/OUTPUT

A computer always has at least one input device, for example, a keyboard, card reader, magnetic tape reader, or paper tape reader, and at

FIGURE 1.1 Principal Components of a Computer

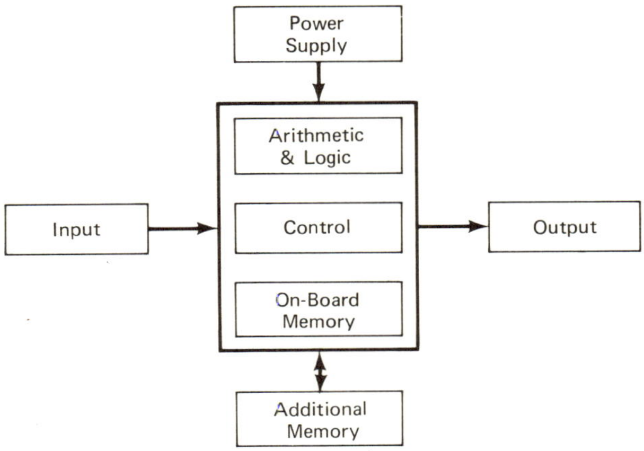

least one output device, such as a teleprinter, magnetic tape, line printer, or visual display unit (VDU).

The ZX81 uses a keyboard and a cassette tape recorder to input information and a television screen to output information. A printer that is compatible with the ZX81 system has also been developed.

CONTROL

The control organizes the execution of the instructions (i.e., program) and the production of results.

ARITHMETIC AND LOGIC

The arithmetic and logic unit is the component that adds, subtracts, multiplies, and divides (arithmetic) and tests for positive, negative, and zero numbers (logic). Although the arithmetic function is fairly obvious, programs need the logic function to decide what action to perform next.

MEMORY

The computer memory is used to store

1. User programs
2. Data
3. System software—program stored permanently in computer memory and used to control the execution of the user programs

The on-board memory consists of 'read-only memory' (ROM) and 'random-access memory' (RAM). ROM is memory which is preprogrammed at manufacture with a permanent program. RAM is general purpose memory in which information may be stored and retrieved when required. RAM loses its contents when power is interrupted, whereas ROM retains its contents.

The memory can be visualized best as a number of storage cells or locations labeled from zero and up. The label of a location is called its address; each storage location is called a word and is subdivided into bits. A bit can contain either a 0 or a 1.

Within the ZX81 memory each word is subdivided into 8 bits and is referred to as a byte (Figure 1.2).

FIGURE 1.2

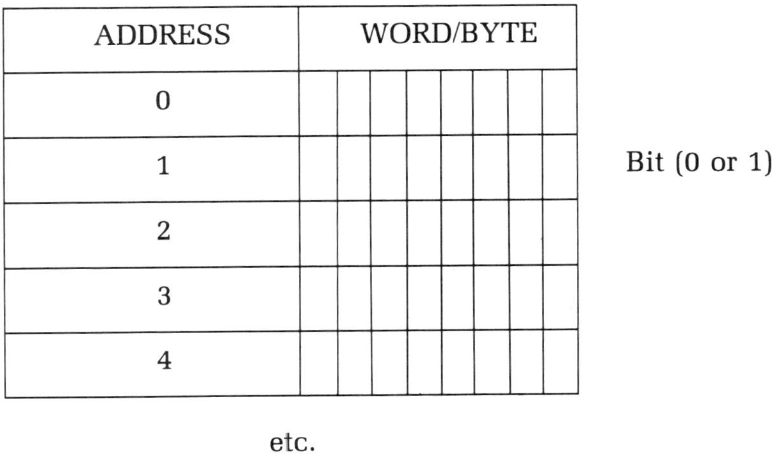

The words are used to store numbers which are interpreted in various ways:

1. A number
2. A character (or a string of characters)
3. An instruction

When a number is stored in a word within the RAM, the previous contents are overwritten and lost for good. When a number is retrieved from the RAM, the contents of the word remain unaltered.

The symbol K is frequently used to represent the quantity of memory available or the quantity of memory required by a program. 1K is equivalent to 1024 (2^{10}) words.

Additional memory can be added to the ZX81 if the on-board memory is insufficient for your job.

NOTATION

Numbers that are stored in words in the form of a pattern of zeros and ones are known as binary numbers. The ZX81, like any other computer, has to use binary notation because it can only distinguish between the two states of a certain component being switched either on or off. An off state is represented by a 0 and an on state by a 1. Thus binary notation is the ideal numbering system for representing data stored in a computer. Humans, however, use the conventional decimal numbering system.

Some programmers become pretty good at using the binary numbering system.

The decimal number 347 is equivalent to

$$(3 \times 10^2) + (4 \times 10^1) + (7 \times 10^0)$$

Likewise a binary number such as 11001 is equivalent to

$$(1 \times 2^4) + (1 \times 2^3) + (0 \times 2^2) + (0 \times 2^1) + (1 \times 2^0)$$
$$= 16 + 8 + 0 + 0 + 1$$
$$= 25 \text{ in decimal}$$

The binary numbering system works similarly to the decimal system. Since more digits are required to express a number in binary than in decimal, the binary system is more cumbersome to use.

When counting with decimal numbers we carry one into the next column to the left every time a nine is reached and the nine is reset to zero.

After 29 The 9 is set to 0 and the 2 is increased to 3 making the next number 30.

After 99 The first 9 on the right is set to 0 and 1 is carried into the next column. The carry over means the second 9 is set to 0 and 1 is carried over into the third column. So the next number is 100.

Similarly, binary numbers carry 1 into the next column every time a 1 is reached and the column is reset back to 0. Thus binary numbers can only contain the digits 0 and 1.

After 1 The first column on the right is set back to 0 and 1 is carried into the next column.

After 10 The first column on the right is increased by 1 so the next number is 11.

After 11 The first column on the right is reset to 0 and 1 is carried into the next column. Since the next column is already 1 it is reset to 0 and 1 is carried into the third column. Therefore the next number is 100.

FIGURE 1.3 Examples of Decimal, Binary, and Hexadecimal Numbers

Decimal.	Binary.	Hex.Dec.	Decimal.	Binary.	Hex.Dec.
+ 1	1	1	−15	11110001	F1
+ 2	10	2	−14	11110010	F2
+ 3	11	3	−13	11110011	F3
+ 4	100	4	−12	11110100	F4
+ 5	101	5	−11	11110101	F5
+ 6	110	6	−10	11110110	F6
+ 7	111	7	− 9	11110111	F7
+ 8	1000	8	− 8	11111000	F8
+ 9	1001	9	− 7	11111001	F9
+10	1010	A	− 6	11111010	FA
+11	1011	B	− 5	11111011	FB
+12	1100	C	− 4	11111100	FC
+13	1101	D	− 3	11111101	FD
+14	1110	E	− 2	11111110	FE
+15	1111	F	− 1	11111111	FF
+16	10000	10	0	00000000	0

Examples of binary numbers are shown in Figure 1.3.

Of course binary numbers can be combined using addition, subtraction, multiplication, and division.

Binary addition uses the following five rules.

$$0 + 0 = 0$$
$$0 + 1 = 1$$
$$1 + 0 = 1$$
$$1 + 1 = 0 \text{ carry } 1$$
$$\text{carry} + 1 + 1 = 1 \text{ carry } 1$$

That is,

1 1 1	Taking first column,	1 + 1	= 0 carry 1
+ 0 1 1	Taking second column,	1 + 1 + carry	= 1 carry 1
1 0 1 0	Taking third column,	1 + carry	= 0 carry 1
1 1 1	Taking fourth column,	carry	= 1

carry
indicators

Binary subtraction uses the following four rules.

0 − 0 = 0
1 − 0 = 1
1 − 1 = 0
0 − 1 = 1 (found by borrowing from next higher digit)

```
  1 0      Taking first column, 0 − 1 is not possible, so bor-
− 0 1                                row from next higher digit
  0 1                                1 0 − 1 = 1
           Taking second column,     0 − 0 = 0
```

```
  1 0 0        borrow indicators        1 0 1
− 0 0 1                               − 0 1 1
  0 1 1                                 0 1 0
```

The computer doesn't just use an on/off state to represent a minus sign. Negative numbers are stored in a form known as *two's complement*. In a word containing x binary bits, − n is stored as $(2^x - n)$. A computer with 8 bits in a word would store

−25 decimal as $2^8 - 25 = 231$

Negative numbers can be visualized as numbers in the opposite direction to positive numbers. For example, if an electric meter reading 0 0 0 0 is wound back one unit it will read 9 9 9 9. To obtain −25 one should wind back 25 units:

9974	9975	9976	....	9997	9998	9999	0	1	2
−26	−25	−24		−3	−2	−1	0	+1	+2

Obtaining the two's complement form can be done simply, in two stages.

1. Obtain the one's complement form by converting the 1's to 0's and vice versa.

Negate 25 decimal.	binary
25 decimal is	0 0 0 1 1 0 0 1
1's complement	1 1 1 0 0 1 1 0
2's complement	1 1 1 0 0 1 1 1

2. The two's complement is found by adding 1 to the one's complement.	So –25 is represented by 1 1 1 0 0 1 1 1
	Negate –25 decimal.
	–25 decimal is 1 1 1 0 0 1 1 1
	1's complement 0 0 0 1 1 0 0 0
	2's complement 0 0 0 1 1 0 0 1
	So –(–25) is represented by 0 0 0 1 1 0 0 1 which is 25 decimal.

If this is a valid form of –25, we would expect 25 + (–25) to be zero.

```
  0 0 0 1 1 0 0 1
 +1 1 1 0 0 1 1 1
 ----------------
1 0 0 0 0 0 0 0 0
```

The last eight digits show this to be so.

The first digit is known as the sign bit. If the sign bit is 0 the number is positive, and if the sign bit is 1 the number is negative. In the case of zero the sign is irrelevant.

In contrast to computers, we humans find these long strings of ones and zeros difficult to memorize and awkward to operate with, so some simpler notations have been developed to help us. One such system uses powers of 16 and is known as the *hexadecimal system* represented by the 16 digits:

0, 1, 2, 3, 4, 5, 6, 7, 8, 9, A, B, C, D, E, F

For example,

$$\begin{aligned} 2F &= (2 \times 16^1) + (F \times 16^0) \\ &= (2 \times 16) + (F \times 1) \\ &= 32 + 15 \\ &= 47 \text{ in decimal} \end{aligned}$$

47 decimal is 101111 in binary so 2F is obviously easier on the eye.

Although some computers appear to work with hexadecimal numbers, the computer still actually stores and operates on them in their binary form.

PROGRAM OPERATION

Now let us consider how a computer copes with a problem. A list of instructions which has been written to solve the problem is entered into the computer. Control will take the instructions and execute them in the order given (right or wrong). The method of solving the problem is known as an *algorithm*. The algorithm is written in a form the computer can understand, known as a *program*. The different forms that a program may be written in are known as languages. Assuming that both the algorithm and language are correct, the computer converts the program into a binary machine code language which can then be executed by the computer.

The formation of algorithms is illustrated in Chapter 2.

We shall now look and see what the ZX81 computer system consists of.

THE SINCLAIR ZX81

The ZX81's central processing unit (CPU) is a Z80A microprocessor which controls all the operations of the computer. The equivalent NEC 780-1 is used interchangeably. To simplify the machine and so reduce the cost, the CPU is also used to drive the display and the cassette interface. The display vanishes when data is being input from either the keyboard or cassette and when data is being processed. There is however a one-quarter speed mode in which the ZX81 computes between the television screen being scanned giving flicker-free animated graphics.

The keyboard is an extremely effective 40-key touch-sensitive membrane. The layout of the keys is the standard 'qwerty' typewriter layout, but the size is much more condensed compared with the majority of keyboards. Entry of characters is by touching rather than tapping the key and since only one key may be touched at a time, experienced touch typists may encounter problems. Any problems disappear with experience.

The display requires an ordinary domestic black and white or color television set. A lead supplied connects the ZX81 to the aerial socket of the television. Reception is received at approximately channel 2 on UHF. The volume of the television is best kept low to avoid any undesirable noise.

The cassette interface for storing programs on tape can be used with almost all domestic cassette recorders. The transfer rate is 250 Baud (unit for bits per second) and uses a unique recording method which is not compatible with other computer systems.

The expansion port is at the rear of the ZX81. It is a 46-pin double-sided edge connector. Signals from this connector can be used for interfacing to other physical units such as additional memory, printer, or one's own electronic projects requiring control, but this is beyond the scope of this book.

The system software is contained in an 8K ROM which contains certain features, notably mathematical functions, that the original ZX80 lacked.

The ZX81 has 1K of internal random-access memory. A large 16K byte pack, which can be added on in one complete module, is available.

The language the ZX81 uses is BASIC (Beginners All-purpose Symbolic Instruction Code). This simple language was designed originally for beginners but has since become the most popular computer language. BASIC is known as a high-level language.

CHAPTER TWO

The Formation of Algorithms

We have looked at the components which are used to make a computer system. The physical parts of the machine are called the *hardware,* while the programs used by the computer instructing the hardware are called the *software.*

Many people have a mistaken idea that computers consist of "brains" that are able to think for themselves. In fact although there are now computers that appear to "talk," "feel," and "see," they are all "helpless" insofar as they can only do what they are told to do. Fortunately, a ZX81 could never revolt and take over the world. The advantages of a computer over a human brain are that it can process information many times faster and it doesn't forget what it has been told.

When a computer program breaks down it is because of an error caused by the programmer. It is essential that a program be unambiguous. It is no use telling a computer to perform some operation on a piece of data if the computer does not know what the data is, or telling the computer to continue at a certain point in the program if this point does not exist. Consider a person telling the decorators to "paint the dining room ceiling—make sure that you cover up the furniture." The decorators will know to protect the furniture before commencing the painting. However, a computer controlled machine would take each instruction in turn, painting the ceiling first and then covering up the furniture.

There are three stages to go through before writing a computer program. First, one must recognize the problem that the computer is required to solve. This is not as trivial as it sounds. Many computer scientists hired to write programs to solve problems find that their employers are not exactly sure of the facts of their problem. Second, what is known as a *mathematical model* has to be produced. This consists of recognizing the important factors that are liable to vary (called *variables*) and finding mathematical relationships between them. Finally the programmer has to use his skill in analyzing the mathematical model to produce an algorithm. Programming skills may be learned and developed by studying other people's software. (Make sure you select good model software.)

It is often easier to plan a program by drawing a diagram, called a flowchart, to represent each operation. Different symbols shown in Figure 2.1 are used to represent each type of operation and the actual procedure is written inside the symbol. The symbols are joined by arrows in the order that control would carry them out.

FIGURE 2.1 Flowchart Symbols

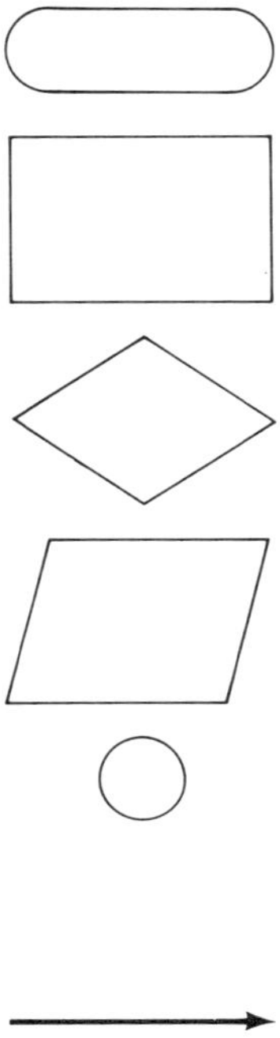

TERMINATOR Used to represent the start or end of a program.

PROCESS Used to represent any operation on data.

DECISION Used to represent a stage where a number of paths can be taken depending on certain conditions.

INPUT/OUTPUT Used to represent the input or output of data.

CONNECTOR Used when a flowchart cannot be completed on a side of paper. Flow continues at a similar connector symbol with the same number inserted in it.

ARROW Direction of flow.

The following flowchart shows the steps in making a cup of coffee.

FIGURE 2.2

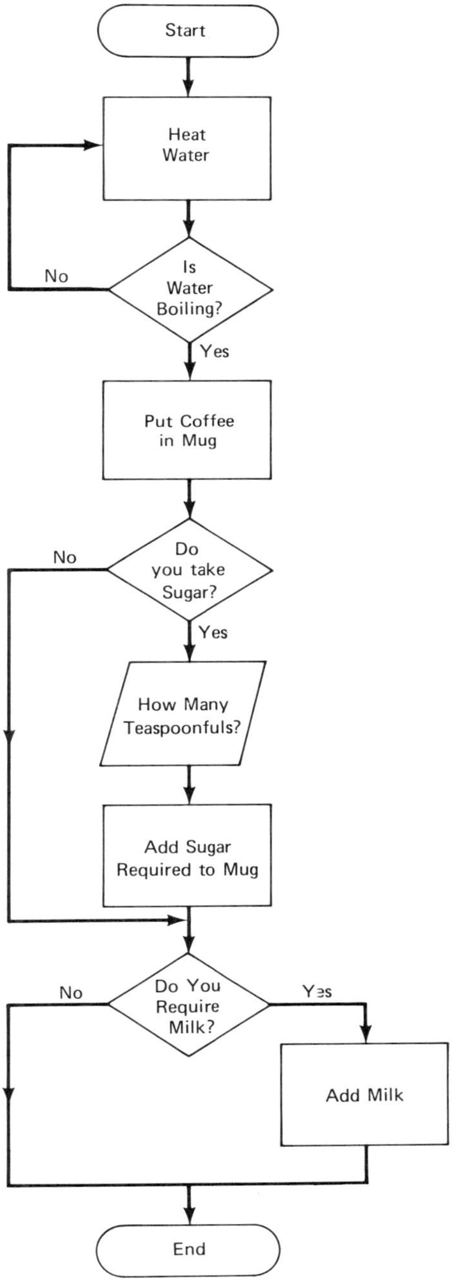

Flowcharts are useful for programs with many decisions and jumps, in which trying to follow just a program listing becomes complicated.

We shall now consider two examples of problems which can be solved by a computer.

I. The addition of two numbers. The important variables are

1. N1 the first number
2. N2 the second number
3. SUM the result of the addition of the two numbers

The mathematical relationship between the variables is simply

SUM = N1 + N2

A simple computer program can be written which inputs the two numbers represented by N1 and N2 and finds the sum, which can then be output.

FIGURE 2.3

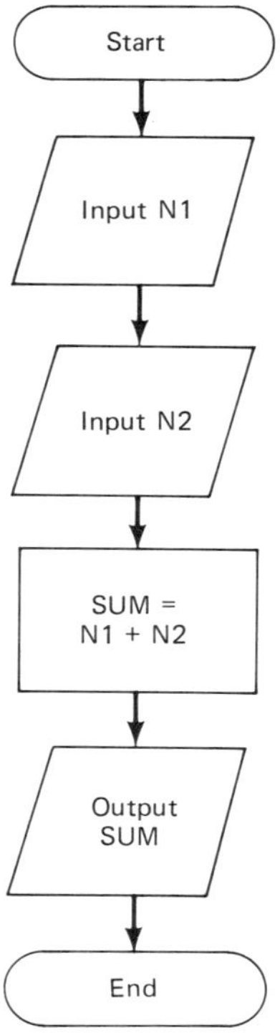

II. The problem of throwing a ball vertically upward with a certain velocity and finding the time taken for the ball to return to the height of its original position. The important variables are

1. U the original velocity of the ball
2. T the time taken
3. S the distance of the ball above the point of throwing
4. A the acceleration due to gravity on the ball

FIGURE 2.4 The Position of a Ball at Time T.

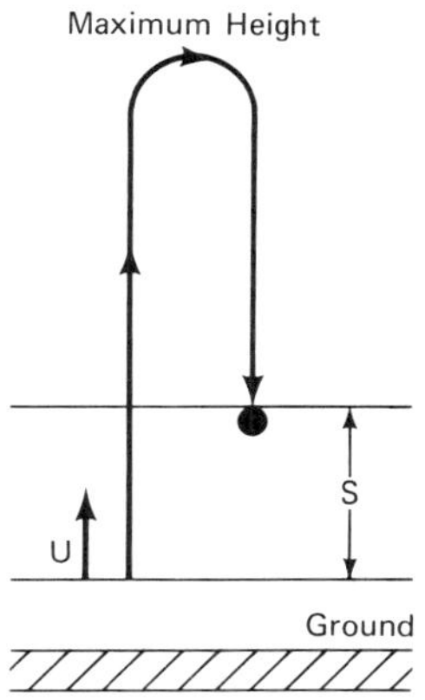

In analyzing the problem several assumptions are made.

1. The acceleration due to gravity is known to be –10 ms $^{-2}$ (–10 meters per second per second). This does in fact vary very slightly depending on the altitude of the ball.
2. Air resistance is neglected.
3. Conditions are ideal, that is, no wind.

Assuming acceleration is constant, by a mathematical technique called integration which is unimportant to a computer user, a formula connecting the important variables can be obtained. This is known to be

$$S = UT + \frac{1}{2}AT^2$$

When the ball returns to its original height S = 0, on substituting S = 0 and A = –10 into the formula we get

$$0 = UT - 5T^2$$

Rearranging we get

$$T = U/5$$

We now have a formula relating the time taken with the initial velocity. This can now be used in a computer program.

The program can be used for any initial velocity required and can be repeated any number of times.

FIGURE 2.5

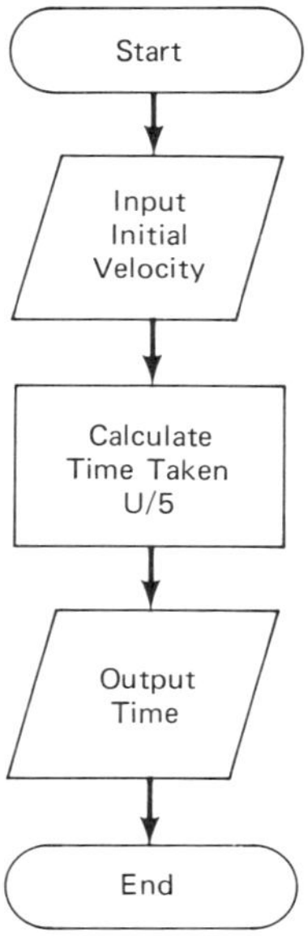

The important thing to remember about a computer is that it can only undertake what the programmer has told it to do and not necessarily what the programmer wants it to do. A program must be 100% correct to produce 100% correct results.

CHAPTER THREE

Introducing the ZX81

OPERATING THE ZX81

There are two connections which have to be made to switch the ZX81 on and start it running:

1. The power supply must be connected to the socket marked 9V DC. The power supply should be 9 volts DC @ 600 mA unregulated.
2. The television aerial socket should be connected to the video socket with the cable provided.

The television should then be tuned to receive the best reception near channel 2. When the screen clears to a steady picture there should be a black square with a white K written on it. This square is known as the *cursor* and indicates the position on the screen where the next character will be entered.

There are two other sockets on the side of the ZX81. These are for saving programs onto a cassette tape, for retrieval at a later date. This is mentioned in more depth under "Saving and Loading" later in this book.

FIGURE 3.1 The ZX81 Computer System

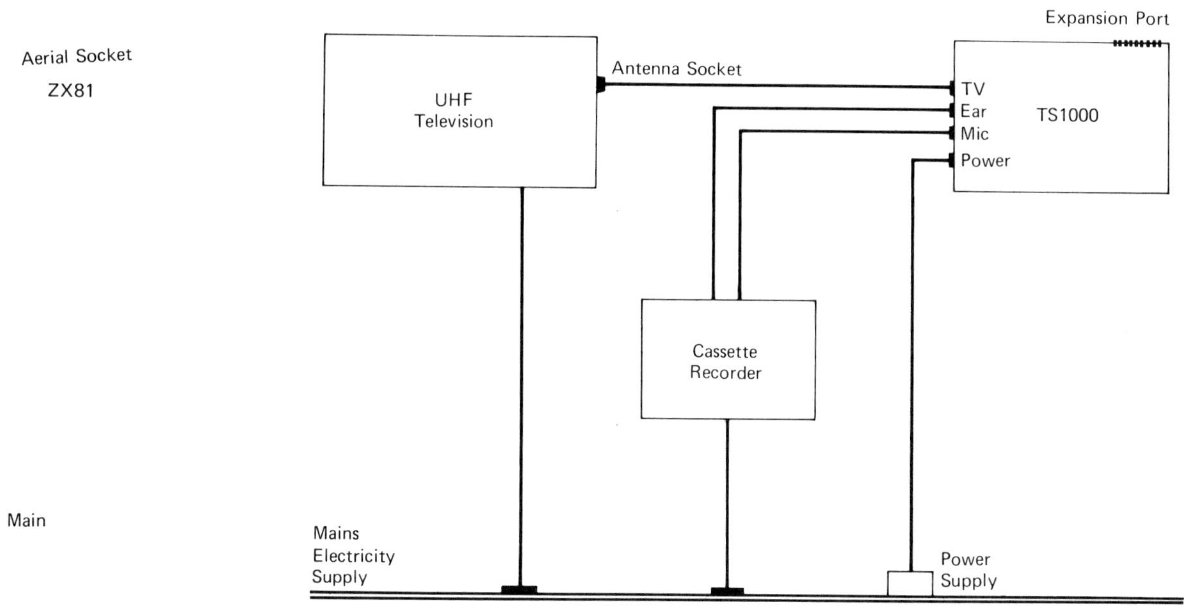

The ZX81 Keyboard

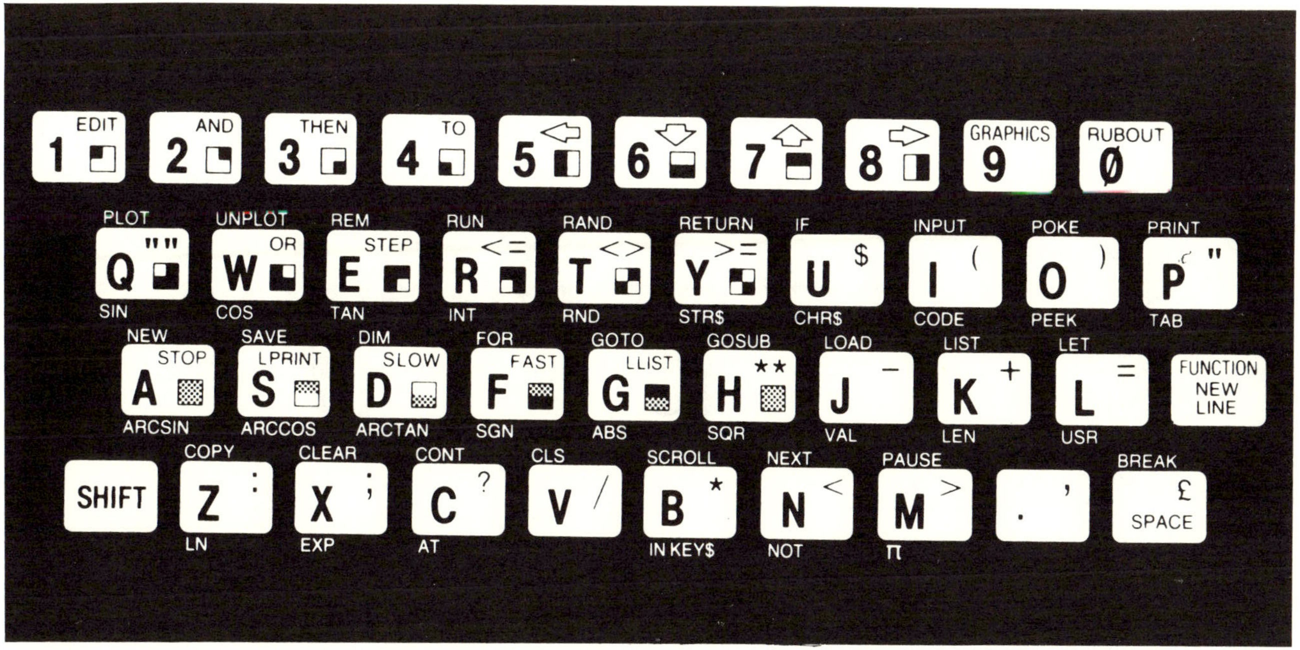

ENTERING A PROGRAM

Consider this simple program of one line.

```
10 PRINT "ZX81"
```

When executed, this will display ZX81 in the top left corner. Enter this program in your ZX81 by pressing the keys shown in Figure 3.2.

The ZX81 is said to be in command mode:

FIGURE 3.2

CURSOR	KEY	DISPLAY
K	1	1
K	0	10
K	P	10 PRINT
L	SHIFT P	10 PRINT "
L	Z	10 PRINT "Z
L	X	10 PRINT "ZX
L	8	10 PRINT "ZX8
L	1	10 PRINT "ZX81
L	SHIFT P	10 PRINT "ZX81"
L	NEW LINE	

As you enter the program, watch the cursor. You will notice when P is pressed, PRINT appears and the cursor changes from [K] to [L]. Note also that a space is automatically displayed on either side of PRINT.

When the cursor is a [K], it expects what is called a *keyword* or a line number. A keyword is a command such as PRINT, RUN, GOTO and is entered by a single keystroke. Keywords are written above the keys on the keyboard. In Figure 3.2, to enter PRINT, since the cursor was [K], the command was entered by simply pressing P. When the cursor has changed to [L], the computer does not expect any more keywords on that line.

When the NEWLINE was pressed, the line appeared at the top of the screen with [>] next to it. This is known as the current line pointer and always points to the last line entered.

To run the program we press R and since the cursor was [K], RUN appears at the base of the screen. Pressing NEWLINE executes the program. The ZX81 is now in program mode. ZX81 appears at the top of the screen with 0 / 10 at the bottom. The 0 tells us the program was executed without any errors and the 10 tells us 10 was the line number of the last line executed. The computer returns to command mode it NEWLINE is pressed.

SYNTAX ERRORS

In the majority of computer systems a program is entered and run, and if there are any errors with the grammar of the program the computer will list the errors. These errors are called *syntax errors*. The ZX81 however has an excellent check for any of these errors. If there is a syntax error on the line being entered, [S] will appear when NEWLINE is pressed. The [S] will indicate the position where the line is syntactically incorrect. A line with a syntax error cannot be entered until the error is corrected. Obviously a check like this can save much time when entering a program for the first time.

In the program to print ZX81, consider the case of leaving the last set of quotation marks off. When NEWLINE is pressed a syntax error cursor appears and the program line cannot be entered at that stage. If the quotation marks are then added, the program line can be entered.

EDITING

The ZX81 has very good facilities for editing one's program. A program will have at the top of the screen a ⊳ pointing to the last line operated on. By pressing both the SHIFT 6 ↓ or SHIFT 7 ↑ simultaneously this cursor can be made to jump either one line down or one line up, respectively. If a certain line is to be edited, the ⊳ must be moved up or down until it points to the line to be changed.

By pressing SHIFT 1 (EDIT), this line appears at the base of the screen. The cursor is present just before the keyword, but can be shifted:

> to the left by SHIFT 5 (left arrow ←) or to the right by SHIFT 8 (right arrow →)

If a character or keyword is to be deleted, move the cursor to the position to the right of it and press SHIFT 0 (RUBOUT). The character or keyword disappears.

If a character is to be added, move the cursor to the position where the character is required and enter the character. Providing the line is syntactically correct, the line can be reentered by pressing NEWLINE.

If a line, which has the same line number as one already within the program, is entered, the new line replaces the old line in the program. The old line is lost for good. Thus lines can be removed from a program by simply typing the line number followed by pressing NEWLINE.

One final use of EDIT is for entering many lines that are similar without having to repeat the typing of each line. For example, suppose lines 100, 200, 300, and 400, were all PRINT "ENTER YOUR STRATEGY 1, 2, or 3" First line 100 is entered . . . by pressing EDIT the line appears at the base of the screen with a single keystroke. By moving the cursor to the left, the 1 can be altered to 2 and the line reentered. This can be repeated for lines 300 and 400, and the result is that the four lines are entered without having to type the same line four times.

It is possible to make the current line pointer point to a certain line by typing:

```
LIST n        (NEWLINE)
```

where n is the number of the line required. This can save time if the pointer is a long way from the line required, or if the line we wish to edit is not on the screen.

CHAPTER FOUR

ZX81 Basic

The ZX81 programming language is just one of the many varieties of the language BASIC. Some statements that are available on other computers are missing on the ZX81, but this can be overcome by the use of one or more of the statements that are available. Similarly, the ZX81 has several statements not found on other computers.

A program is made up of lines each containing one instruction preceded by a line number in the range of 1 to 9999. The program statements are displayed in the order of their line numbers and this is the order in which they are executed. Thus if a line is required to be inserted between two lines already in the program, the new line must have a number that is between the two line numbers in the program.

VARIABLES

All pieces of data stored in the ZX81 memory in a BASIC program are labeled by symbolic names which refer to the cell where the data is stored. If we wrote a statement such as

```
5  INPUT A
```

the control would reserve a cell in the memory and from then on A would refer to the data stored in that particular cell. Since the data stored in a cell can be changed, these names are known as variables.

Certain rules govern choosing names for cells. Variables which can store numbers can have variable names of any length and consist of both alphabetic and numeric characters, providing the name starts with a letter. Strings of characters can be stored in string variables whose names have the form of a single alphabetic character followed by the symbol $.

VALID VARIABLE names include

Number variable	A
Number variable	A1
Number variable	AB
Number variable	MAX
String variable	A$
String variable	R$

INVALID VARIABLE names include

Number variable	2A	(does not start with a letter)
Number variable	A B	(space not allowed within variable name)
Number variable	A.B	(characters other than alphabetic or numeric not allowed in variable name)
String variable	2$	(must start with alphabetic character)
String variable	A2$	(too many characters preceding $)
String variable	MIN$	(too many characters preceding $)

NUMBERS

The ZX81 is capable of recognizing three different types of numbers.

1. Integers These numbers which are a sequence of decimal digits and no decimal point appears:

    1, 2, 10, –150, –5, 0000

2. Real A sequence of decimal digits with a single decimal point either at the end, beginning, or between two digits:

    5.6, –2.7, 3.0, –1.5, .4, 5

3. Exponential This scientific notation is useful for storing either very small or very large numbers and consists of a number in front of an E and an integer after it. The E signifies *times ten to the power of:*

12.6E2	=	12.6×10^{2}	=	1260.0
12.6E0	=	12.6×10^{0}	=	12.6
12.6E–2	=	12.6×10^{-2}	=	0.126

The effect of the integer after the E is to tell how many places the decimal point is to be shifted. A positive integer means shift to the right and a negative integer means shift to the left.

The largest number, that is, the number farthest away from zero, that the ZX81 is capable of storing is approximately $\pm 1 * 10^{38}$, the smallest number, the nearest to zero, is approximately $\pm 3 * 10^{-39}$. The ZX81 stores numbers to an accuracy of between nine and ten digits.

ALGEBRAIC EXPRESSIONS

An algebraic expression is a list of variable names or numbers known as operands linked together by any of the following operators.

1. + addition
2. – subtraction
3. * multiplication
4. / division
5. ** raised to the power of
6. – negation

For example,

A + B * C * 6 * A
–A * B + 3.0 – C
A ** B
A/B

Note the difference between negation and subtraction. Subtraction operates on two operands, A – B, whereas negation operates on one operand, –C.

Brackets are also allowed in algebraic expressions, in which case the algebraic expression inside the bracket would be evaluated first:

A + 5 / (B + A)

Now consider the expression

A + B * C

The computer could interpret this in two ways.

1. C multiplied by the result of A plus B
2. A added to the result of B multiplied by C

Therefore there must be some rules on giving the order that the operands are operated on.

Each operator is given a value known as its hierarchy or priority as shown in Figure 4.1. The computer first considers all operators with the highest priority and evaluates them from left to right. It then considers the operators with the second highest priority and evaluates them from left to right. This continues until the whole expression has been evaluated.

FIGURE 4.1 Hierarchy of the ZX81 Operators

OPERATOR	PRIORITY
**	10
–n	9
*	8
/	8
+	6
–	6

To demonstrate:

−4 + 3 ** 2 * 6 − 4 * 9 / 12	
	Priority 10
−4 + 9 * 6 − 4 * 9 / 12	
	Priority 9
−4 + 9 * 6 − 4 * 9 / 12	
	Priority 8
−4 + 54 − 3	
	Priority 6
47	

CHAPTER FIVE

Statements

As already mentioned, a basic program is a list of numbered lines containing statements. A statement can do two things. It may either just state something or it may tell the computer to do some operation. We now deal with the statements available on the ZX81. These statements can be subdivided into several catagories:

1. System commands   not usually used in a program but are used in operating the computer
2. Assignment statements   used to assign a particular value to certain variables
3. Input/output statements   used for the input and the output of data
4. Control statements   used to control the sequence in which other program statements are executed
5. Other statements and functions

SYSTEM COMMANDS

The following keywords are system commands. They may be used in a program but this use is very limited. (n) represents an integer that may follow the command, if required.

CLEAR [K] [X] Clears all variables thus releasing their space in the computer memory. The program is unaltered.

CONT [K] [C] Restarts a program from the line where the execution of the program last finished. If execution had stopped due to a STOP statement the program will restart at the line immediately after this line.

LIST (n) [K] [K] Lists the program from line n on the television screen and sets current line pointer to line n. If n is omitted then the program will be listed from the start.

LLIST (n) [K] or [L] [SHIFT] [G] Like LIST but uses printer, if attached, instead of the television screen.

LOAD "name" [K] [J] Loads program called "name" and its variables from cassette tape.

NEW [K] [A] Clears computer memory of both program and variables.

RUN (n) [K] [R] Clears variables and executes program from line n. If n is omitted the program will be executed from the start.

SAVE "name" [K] [S] Records programs called "name" and its variables on to cassette tape.

The following terms are not keywords but are still used for controlling the computer and its programs.

BREAK [SPACE] Halts the program under execution and returns computer to command mode.

EDIT [K] or [L] [SHIFT] [1] Returns line pointed to by current line pointer for editing.

FUNCTION [K] or [L] [SHIFT] [NEWLINE] This enables the certain functions (which will be discussed later in more depth) to be entered. When FUNCTION is pressed the cursor changes to [F] and control will expect a function which is printed beneath the appropriate key.

GRAPHIC [G], [K] or [L] [SHIFT] [9] This enables inverse characters, that is white characters on a black background, and the pixel graphics, which are squares shaded in various patterns, to be entered. When GRAPHIC is pressed, the cursor will change from either [K] or [L] to [G]. Now pressing a key causes the inverse characters to be entered. The pixel graphics are accessible by pressing SHIFT simultaneously with the required key. Pressing GRAPHIC again will return the cursor back to the original [K] or [L].

NEWLINE [NEWLINE] Enters statement at base of screen.

RUBOUT [G], [K] or [L] [SHIFT] [0] Deletes character or keyword to left of cursor.

ASSIGNMENT STATEMENTS

LET [K] 

The syntax of the LET statement is of the following form:

Line number   LET integer variable = algebraic expression.
Line number   LET string variable = string expression.

The LET statement assigns the value of the expression to the variable specified. For example,

1. 10 LET A = 100
   This assigns a value of 100 to the variable A.
2. 10 LET B = B + 2
   This assigns the value of variable B plus 2 back into B. B is incremented by 2.
3. 10 LET Z$ = "ZX81"
   This assigns the string of characters ZX81 to Z$.
4. 10 LET Z$ = "SINCLAIR" + "ZX81"
   This assigns the string of characters SINCLAIRZX81 to Z$ and is an example of concatenation. However, strings may not be subtracted, multiplied, divided, or raised to a power.

INPUT AND OUTPUT STATEMENTS

INPUT [K] 

The syntax of the INPUT statement is of the form:

line number INPUT variable

When control comes across an INPUT statement, the program will halt and require some data to be input through the keyboard. For example,

1. 5 INPUT A
   This will request numerical data to be entered.
2. 5 INPUT A$
   This will request string data to be entered.

If numerical data is required, a cursor [L] appears at the base of the screen. If string data is required a cursor [L] is within a pair of quotation marks. The entering of characters when numerical data is wanted will cause an

TRIGONOMETRIC FUNCTIONS

The ZX81 has six trigonometric functions called SIN, COS, TAN, ARCSIN, ARCCOS, and ARCTAN. Note that all angles are measured in radians, so if degrees are required, results must be converted.

1 radian is the angle subtended by an arc on a circle of the same length as its radius.

To convert radians into degrees multiply by

$$\frac{180}{\pi}$$

where π is approximately 3.141592653 and is written as PI. Thus

$$\frac{PI}{3} \text{ radians} = \frac{PI}{3} * \frac{180}{PI} = 60°$$

PI is accessible on the ZX81 as a function without an argument. [F] [M]

FIGURE 6.1

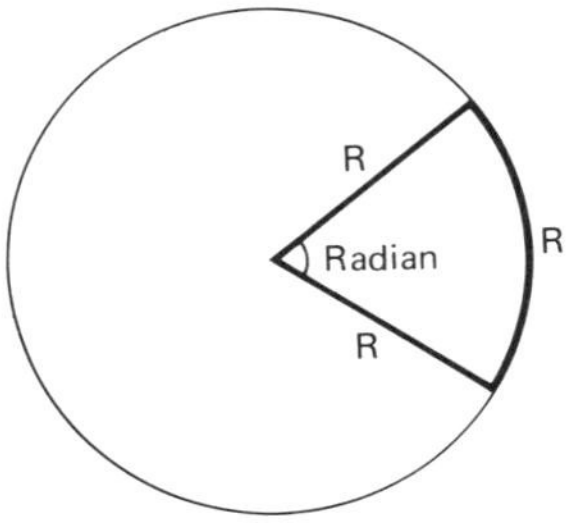

error while the entering of numbers when a string is required is perfectly proper since the digits can be accepted as characters.

The INPUT statement is also useful for temporarily stopping a program in order that the screen is displayed. It is often best in this case to request the input of a string since the program can be continued by the single keystroke of NEWLINE.

PRINT [K]

The PRINT statement is used to output information by displaying it on the screen. It is followed by the print items which can take various forms:

1. 10 PRINT A
   The value of variable A is displayed provided it exists.
2. 10 PRINT A$
   The value of variable A$ is displayed provided it exists.
3. 10 PRINT "AVERAGE"
   AVERAGE is displayed.
4. 10 PRINT 2 * 5 + 4
   The expression is calculated and displayed.
5. 10 PRINT
   A blank line is displayed.

It is also possible to printout a combination of the above with one PRINT statement. Each item must be separated by either ; or , . A semicolon between two items causes the printing of a second item to follow on immediately after the first. A comma between two items causes the print position for the second item to be shifted on at least one place, so that it starts at either the center column on the screen (column 16) or on the next line (column 0).

6. 10 PRINT "AVERAGE "; (A + B) / 2
   AVERAGE is displayed followed by the result of the expression.
7. 10 PRINT A, B
   Contents of A and B are displayed in the columns 0 and 16 respectively.

COPY [K] A copy of the display is sent to the printer. If the printer is not attached, nothing will happen.

LPRINT [K] or [L] Like PRINT, but if the printer is attached to the computer it will print there instead of on the screen.

CONTROL STATEMENTS

GOTO [K]

With this instruction it is possible to alter the usual sequence in which control processes the numbered statements. The syntax of the GOTO statement is of the following forms:

1. Line number GOTO n (where n is an integer)
   Control will jump to line n if it exists otherwise the first line after n.
2. Line number GOTO algebraic expression
   Control will jump to the line whose number is the result of the algebraic expression.

When in command mode it is possible to execute a program by pressing

```
GOTO n
```

where n is the line number that control is to commence at. This method differs from RUN in that the variables are not cleared before execution.

Now let us look at a simple program using the INPUT, PRINT, and GOTO statements which will produce some interesting patterns.

Program 1—Patterns

```
 5 INPUT A$
10 PRINT A$;
15 GOTO 10
```

RUN the program and enter between three and six graphic characters followed by NEWLINE.

The string of characters is assigned to string variable A$. A$ is then printed and control is sent back to line 10 and so printed again. This continues until the whole screen is filled. By rerunning the program, a different set of characters can be entered and a different pattern produced. Entering four characters causes vertical patterns while entering three, five, or six characters causes diagonal patterns.

PROGRAM 1 Patterns

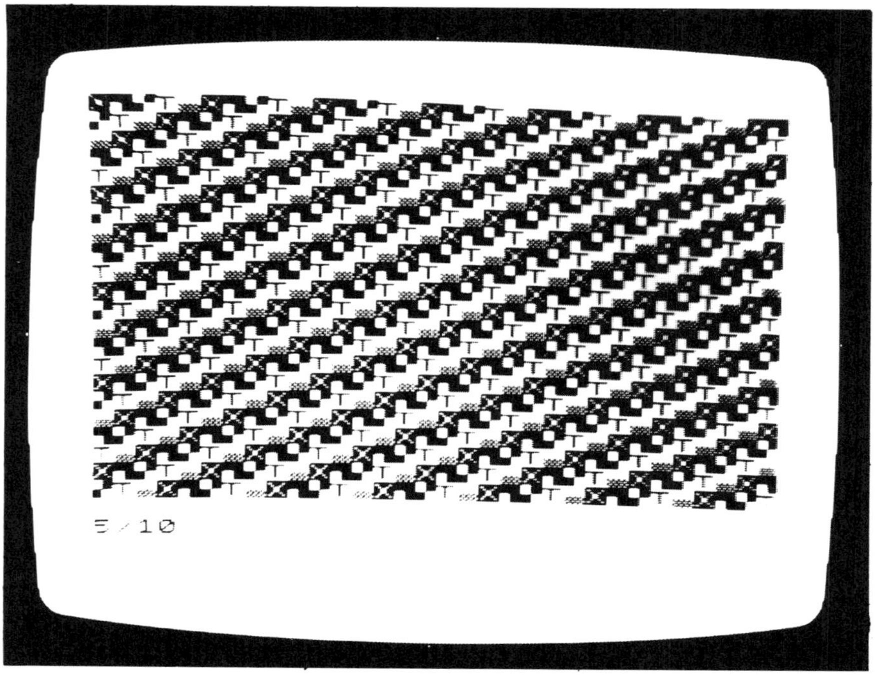

FOR-NEXT [K] [F], [K] [N]

The syntax of this useful loop takes the following form:

```
FOR Φ = x TO y STEP z
. . . . . )
. . . . . }    (section of program to be looped)
. . . . . )
NEXT Φ
```

where Φ is any number variable of a single letter and is known as the control variable and x, y, and z are algebraic expressions.

TO and STEP are not keywords but are called tokens and are obtained by pressing their key simultaneously with SHIFT. That is

[K] or [L] SHIFT 4 (TO)

[K] or [L] SHIFT 3 (THEN)

Φ is initially assigned the value of x and the program section is executed until NEXT Φ is found. Control now jumps back to the FOR statement and Φ is incremented by a value z.

If z is greater than zero this looping will continue until Φ is greater than y, in which case control continues at the statement after NEXT Φ.

If z is less than zero this looping continues until Φ is less than y. For example,

```
 5 FOR J = 1 TO 10 STEP 1
10 PRINT J;
15 NEXT J
```

This causes numbers 1 to 10 to be displayed.

```
 5 FOR J = 10 TO 1 STEP -1
10 PRINT J;
15 NEXT J
```

This causes numbers 10 to 1 to be displayed.

If the value of z is +1 we can simplify the statement by just writing

```
FOR Φ = x TO y
```

FOR loops can be nested inside each other provided they do not cross into each other.

```
FOR 1
NEXT 1
```

```
FOR 1
FOR 2
FOR 3
NEXT 3
NEXT 2
NEXT 1
```

```
FOR 1
FOR 2
NEXT 2
FOR 3
NEXT 3
NEXT 1
```

The above examples are perfect.

```
FOR 1
FOR 2
NEXT 1
NEXT 2
```

This however causes all sorts of problems and should be avoided.

FOR loops can be jumped out of before a control value has reached its terminating value; however, they should never be jumped into.

The following program demonstrates FOR loops by displaying a flag similar to a "Star Spangled Banner" on the screen.

```
     ┌──►10  FOR I = 1 TO 5
     │ ┌►15  FOR J = 1 TO 10
     │ J  20  PRINT "*";  ◄──── (inverse multiplication symbol)
     │ └─25  NEXT J
     I ┌►30  FOR J = 1 TO 15
     │ J  35  PRINT "▨";
     │ └─40  NEXT J
     │    45  PRINT
     └───50  NEXT I
     ┌──►55  FOR I = 1 TO 6
     │ ┌►60  FOR J = 1 TO 25
     I J  65  PRINT "▨";
     │ └─70  NEXT J
     │    75  PRINT
     └───80  NEXT I
```

IF-THEN [K] , [K] or [L] 

This powerful statement enables the computer to make decisions. The syntax of the IF / THEN statement is of the form:

line number IF condition THEN statement

If the condition is true, the statement is executed; otherwise control continues the program on the next line. The statement may be any of the available conditions commencing with a keyword. The condition consists of two algebraic expressions or two string expressions separated by one of the following relations:

= ..... Equal to
< ..... Less than
<= ..... Less than or equal to
> ..... Greater than
>= ..... Greater than or equal to
<> ..... Not equal to

1. A + B = C / 2
   A plus B equal to one-half of C.
2. A <> 100
   A not equal to one hundred.
3. A > B * 2
   A greater than two multiplied by B.
4. Q$ = "YES"
   Q$ equal to string of characters YES.

String variables must not be compared with numerical expressions. When comparing strings a string is found to be less than another if it comes first in alphabetical order.

```
 A  < Z
AA  < AZ
A□  < AA
□A  < AA
□A  < A□
 1  < 9
K2  < K9
```

An example of the IF statement is illustrated in Program 2.

The ZX81 can be used as a data bank—that is, for storing and retrieving information such as telephone numbers, addresses, birthdays, and so on. The data is programmed into the ZX81 and may be stored on tape until required. Program 2 is one of the many ways of storing this type of data and enables just the required section of data to be accessed quickly.

Program 2—Data Bank

```
 5 PRINT "TELEPHONE NUMBERS"
10 INPUT N$
15 PRINT N$
20 IF N$ = "KERMIT" THEN PRINT "FROGMORE 1111"
25 IF N$ = "SINCLAIR" THEN PRINT "0276 66104"
30 IF N$ = "name 3" THEN PRINT "telephone no.3"
35 IF N$ = "name 4" THEN PRINT "telephone no.4"
40 IF N$ = "name 5" THEN PRINT "telephone no.5"
45 ...... ETC.
```

The examples of names and telephone numbers can be replaced by ones required.

A program like this is very useful when used with a 16K memory expansion where larger quantities of data may be stored.

STOP [K] or [L] SHIFT A (NEW / STOP / ARCSIN)

This stops the execution of the program.

GOSUB-RETURN [K] H (GOSUB / ** / SQR), [K] Y (RETURN / >= / STR$)

In a program there may be a section which is repeated several times. Instead of keeping on reproducing the same section it may be written once and called for when required. This section of a program is called a subroutine.

To implement a subroutine write

line number GOSUB n

where n is the line number where the subroutine commences. At the end of a subroutine write

line number RETURN

and this tells control to return to line immediately after the line which called the subroutine.

```
 10 GOSUB 100  }
 20 GOSUB 100  }
 30 GOSUB 100  }  main program
 40 GOSUB 100  }
 50 STOP       }
100 PRINT "SUBROUTINE CALLED"  }
110 RETURN                     }  subroutine
```

In the example above the subroutine starting at line 100 is called four times.

Note it is important never to let the program run through a subroutine by accident. In the example shown a STOP statement is used at the end of the main program to prevent this happening.

A subroutine may also call another subroutine. A subroutine that calls itself is said to be *recursive*.

OTHER STATEMENTS

CLS [K] 

When control executes this statement, the screen is cleared. The syntax of the statement is

line number CLS

If the screen is not cleared when it becomes full, any attempt to display information on the next line will cause an error.

REM [K] 

REM (Remark) statements are not executed by the computer but are used to clarify sections of a program to the reader. The syntax of the statement is

line number REM message

That is, 10 REM INITIALIZE TO ZERO
Control ignores line 10 and continues from the next line.

PAUSE [K] 

PAUSE causes the execution of the program to halt temporarily for a specified time or until any key is pressed. The syntax of the statement is

line number PAUSE n

where the execution is required to halt for n/60th seconds. That is,

100 PAUSE 120

will cause a halt of two seconds.
n must be in the range 0 < = n < = 65535 or an error will occur. If n > = 32767 the delay is not timed but lasts until any key is pressed.

SCROLL [K] 

SCROLL causes the display to be scrolled up the screen one line, with the top line vanishing and a blank line appearing at the base of the screen.

The syntax of the statement is

line number SCROLL

DIM K 

It is often required to reserve a block of cells known as an array within the memory that can be referred to by a name (referring to the block) and a number (referring to the cell). Control is instructed to reserve such a block of a particular length by the DIM (dimension) statement.
The syntax of the statement is

line number DIM name (length)

where the name is a single letter only. That is,

```
10 DIM A(8)
```

tells the computer to reserve a block of eight cells which will be called A.

A(1)	A(2)	A(3)	A(4)	A(5)	A(6)	A(7)	A(8)

Each cell is capable of storing a number. When the block is declared, each cell is initialized to zero. One may refer to any cell required by, for example, cell 5, using the name A(5). The term in brackets is called the subscript. The same cell could be referred to by A(J) if J was equal to 5. Also, A (algebraic expression) is valid [A(2 * I + 6)], but the subscript must be in the range specified by the DIM statement or an error will occur.

It is also possible to set up arrays with more than one subscript. That is,

```
10 DIM B(3,3)
```

will reserve a block of nine cells.

B(1,1)	B(1,2)	B(1,3)
B(2,1)	B(2,2)	B(2,3)
B(3,1)	B(3,2)	B(3,3)

This is known as a two-dimensional array. The same idea works for an n-dimensional array.

It is possible to have string character arrays where each cell is capable of storing a single character. That is,

```
10 DIM A$(3,6)
```

reserves eighteen cells in a block of three cells by six cells. Three strings of six or fewer characters could be stored in this block:

```
10 DIM A$(3,6)
15 LET A$(1) = "MORGAN"
20 LET A$(2) = "VOLVO"
25 LET A$(3) = "PORSCHE"
```

causes the block to store

	1	2	3	4	5	6
1	M	O	R	G	A	N
2	V	O	L	V	O	
3	P	O	R	S	C	H

There are two important points to notice in this example. First, the second subscript in the assignment statements was omitted; when this happens the computer assumes a fixed length string, in this example of six characters. Second, in line 20 the string "VOLVO" was fewer than six characters so a space was automatically added to make up the difference. Likewise in line 25, the string "PORSCHE" was greater than six characters so the last character was ignored.

We can also take a subsection of a string known as a *slice*. For example,

```
30 PRINT A$(3,4 TO 6)
```

causes A$(3,4);A$(3,5);A$(3,6) to be printed.

Program 3 illustrates slices being used. A sentence of English is entered and then printed out with all four letter words blotted out.

Program 3—The Mary Whitehouse Program

```
 5 DIM A$(60)
10 INPUT A$(2 TO 59)
15 FOR J = 1 TO 55
20 IF  A$(J)<> "□" THEN GOTO 45
25 FOR K = 1 TO 4
30 IF A$(J + K) = "□" THEN GOTO 45
35 NEXT K
40 IF A$(J + 5) = "□"
          THEN LET A$(J + 1 TO J + 4) = "****"
45 PRINT A$(J);
50 NEXT J
```

An array containing 60 character cells is set up, but the INPUT statement just fills 58 of them, leaving the first and last with a blank space. A pointer J is set up to move from 1 to 55 representing each cell in turn. The computer first checks that the cell J points to is a blank cell, then that the next four cells are all characters and finally that the next cell is another blank. If it is found all those conditions were true a four-letter word is present and so this subsection of the string must be replaced by four stars as in line 40. If it is found that these conditions were not true J is increased by one and the next set of six characters are considered. For example,

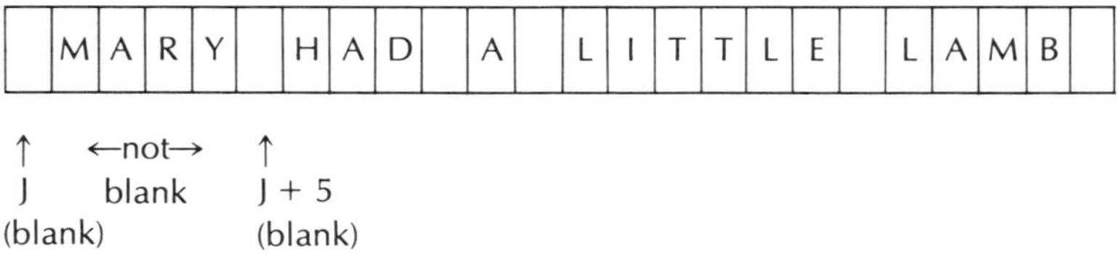

Cells J+1, J+2, J+3, J+4 must be replaced by four stars and this is achieved by LET A$(J + 1 TO J +4) = "****"

Program 4 stores up to 20 strings of a maximum 10 characters in an array called A$ and then sorts them into alphabetical order.

Program 4—Alphabetical Sorting

```
 5 INPUT N
10 DIM A$(N,10)
15 FOR J = 1 TO N
20 INPUT A$(J)
25 NEXT J
30 FOR J = 2 TO N
35 LET T$ = A$(J)
40 FOR I = J - 1 TO 1 STEP -1
45 IF A$(I) < T$ THEN GOTO 60
50 LET A$(I + 1) = A$(I)
55 NEXT I
60 LET A$(I + 1) = T$
65 NEXT J
70 FOR J = 1 TO N
75 PRINT A$(J)
80 NEXT J
```

RUN the program. First input the number of strings to be sorted and then input each string in turn. After the last string is entered, they are sorted and printed in alphabetical order.

The program takes each string in turn starting at the second and moves it up the array until it is in a position such that its numerical value is between the values of the string above and below. The overall result is to put the strings in order so that their values are increasing.

Consider the strings ZZ, ZA, X, ZB, C to be sorted.

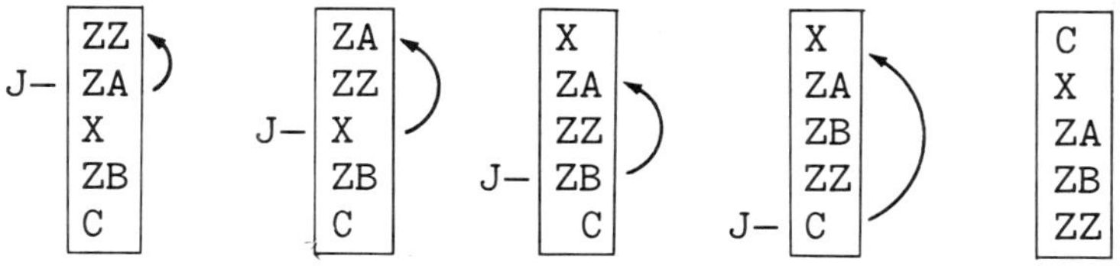

This method of sorting is sometimes called a bubble sort because the lowest values "float" upwards and the highest values "sink" to the bottom.

If the memory expansion is connected you can sort a larger number of strings, but you must arrange the printing of the results so that the screen is not overfilled. The bubble sort is an ideal method for small quantities of data (fewer than 75) but there are better algorithms for sorting vast quantities.

SLOW & FAST [K] or [L] SHIFT D

[K] or [L] SHIFT F

When the ZX81 is first switched on it displays the information on the television and "thinks" between the scanning of the screen. The ZX81 is said to be in SLOW mode.

It is however possible to make the ZX81 operate four times faster by letting it ignore the screen while it is "thinking." Then the ZX81 is said to be in FAST mode.

When in command mode it is possible to switch speeds by pressing either FAST or SLOW depending on which is required. FAST or SLOW may also be put into a program. There is no restriction on the number of times you can switch from one mode to another. Owners of a ZX80 with the 8K ROM will find their computers only function in FAST mode.

There is no definite rule when each speed should be used although FAST is usually best kept for when you have many numerical calculations and the speed of calculation is more important than what the screen looks like. Sometimes FAST is preferred in command mode when entering a long program as when each line is entered the program listing is built up from the start and this can be very time consuming.

To compare the two modes, experiment with a program like the alphabetical sorting program using the same data but first in SLOW mode and second in FAST mode.

The other statements that are mentioned later when required are RAND, PLOT, UNPLOT, and POKE.

CHAPTER SIX

The ZX81 Functions

A function is a rule that returns a value, usually by replacing another number known as the argument. The ZX81 has a series of functions available which are written below their associated key and are accessible by first pressing [SHIFT] [FUNCTION NEW LINE]. The cursor changes to [F]. This indicates that the computer expects a function.

RND (Random Number Generator) [F] [T / RAND / RND]

The random number generator is useful and extremely desirable for certain games. The generator is really a long sequence of numbers, but this is usually more than adequate for most needs of the user. This is known as a pseudorandom number generator.

RND gives a random number greater or equal to zero but less than one. For example,

```
10 LET A = RND
```

assigns a number in the range 0 < = x < 1 to variable A.

It is possible to get the computer to commence the sequence of random numbers at the same place every time by using the statement RAND [K] [T / RAND / RND]. For example,

```
5 RAND n
```

(where n is known as the seed)

RND always returns the same value after executing RAND with a particular value. To obtain a random seed and hence start the sequence of random numbers in an unknown position use either RAND 0 or RAND which sets the seed to the number of times the television screen has been scanned since the ZX81 was switched on.

INT (Integer component) [F] 

This function returns the integer component of the argument by rounding down.

```
10 PRINT INT -5.6
15 PRINT INT 0
20 PRINT INT 5.6
```

This causes –6, 0 and 5 to be printed.

The next few programs show examples of the use of RND and INT.

The function INT is used in Program 5, which finds the highest common factor of two positive integers (the largest number that is a factor of each of the entered numbers).

Program 5—Highest Common Factor

```
 5 PRINT "ENTER FIRST NUMBER ";
10 INPUT A
15 PRINT A, "ENTER SECOND NUMBER ";
20 INPUT B
25 PRINT B
30 LET C = B
35 LET B = A - B * INT (A/B)
40 LET A = C
45 IF B <> 0 THEN GOTO 30
50 PRINT "HIGHEST COMMON FACTOR "; C
```

Try to follow the program on paper by drawing three columns labeled A, B, and C. Record the value of each variable in the corresponding column as it is changed.

Program 6—Dice

```
 5 RAND
10 LET T = 0
15 DIM A(6)
20 PRINT "DICE"
25 FOR I = 1 TO 48
30 LET B = INT (RND * 6 + 1)
35 LET A(B) = A(B) + 1
40 LET T = T + B
45 PRINT B; "□";
50 NEXT I
55 PRINT "RESULTS"
60 FOR I = 1 TO 6
65 PRINT I; ".."; A(I)
70 NEXT I
75 PRINT "TOTAL  ";T
```

Program 6 represents a die being thrown 48 times. It also displays how many times each value on the die is obtained and the total of all the throws.

A random integer from 1 to 6 is obtained by using

```
INT (RND * 6 + 1)
```

The number of times a value is thrown is recorded by adding 1 to the corresponding cell in the array A(6). A running total is kept in variable T.

Program 7—Multiplication Test

```
 5 RAND
10 LET S = 0
15 FOR I = 1 TO 20
20 CLS
25 LET M = 2 + INT (RND * 11)
30 LET N = 2 + INT (RND * 11)
35 PRINT "QUESTION  ";I
40 PRINT
45 PRINT M; " * "; N; " = ";
50 INPUT Q
55 PRINT M * N
60 IF Q = M * N THEN PRINT "WELL DONE"
65 IF Q = M * N THEN LET S = S + 1
70 PAUSE 100
75 NEXT I
80 CLS
85 PRINT "SCORE  "; S; " /20"
```

Program 7 asks 20 questions on the multiplication tables. After the twentieth question the computer displays how many questions were answered correctly.

Lines 25 and 30 select two random integers from 2 to 12 and assign them to M and N. The question is then displayed and the answer requested. If the answer is equal to M * N then the score S is incremented by 1 and "WELL DONE" is printed. A pause is included so that the user can study the answer before the computer asks the next question.

Program 8—What Day?

```
  5 LET A$ = "SUNMONTUEWEDTHUFRISAT"
 10 CLS
 15 PRINT "DATE  ";
 20 INPUT D
 25 PRINT D,, "MONTH  ";
 30 INPUT M
 35 PRINT M,,"YEAR  ";
 40 INPUT Y
 45 PRINT Y
 50 LET M = M - 2
 55 IF M > 0 THEN GOTO 70
 60 LET M = M + 12
 65 LET Y = Y - 1
 70 LET C = INT (Y/100)
 75 LET Y = Y-100 * C
 80 LET F = D + INT (2.6 * M - .19) + Y
              + INT (Y/4) + INT (C/4) - 2 * C
 85 LET F = F - 7 * INT (F/7)
 90 PRINT   A$ (F * 3 + 1 TO F * 3 + 3)
 95 INPUT B$
100 IF B$ = "" THEN GOTO 10
```

Program 8 responds to any given calendar date by printing out the day of the week that the date fell on. The original calendar was devised by Julius Caesar but he fixed the length of year by 11 minutes too long. This error was rectified by the Gregorian calendar in Italy in 1582, although this was not introduced in England until 1752. The program will not give correct answers for dates before this.

Enter a date in digital form, for instance, May 6, 1961 would be

```
   6 NEWLINE
   5 NEWLINE
1961 NEWLINE
```

Do not try to follow the mathematics in the program, but notice how the function INT is used to round numbers down to the nearest integer. Line 85 eventually produces a result in the range 0 to 6 where 0 represents Sunday, 1 represents Monday and so on up to 6 representing Saturday. Line 90 prints out the corresponding slice of A$ giving the required day of the week.

SIN x [F] 

SIN x is defined as the ratio of the length of the opposite side to the hypotenuse in a right-angled triangle with an angle of x radians.

FIGURE 6.2

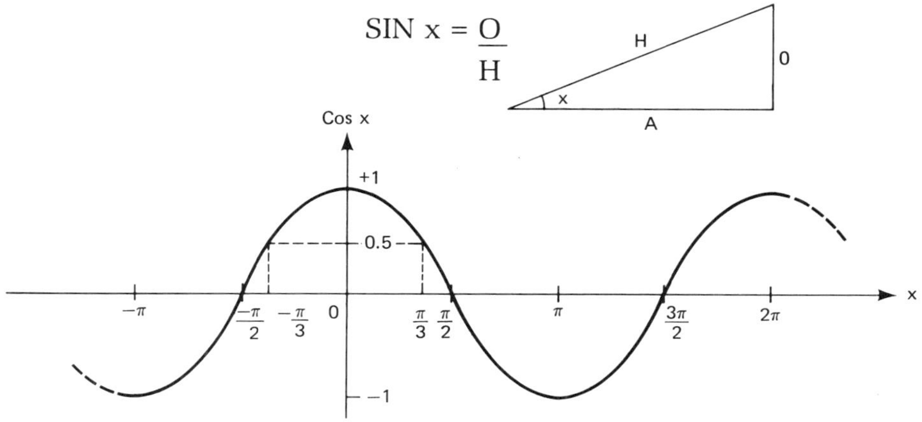

ARCSIN y [F] 

ARCSIN y is the angle whose SIN is y.

COS x [F] 

COS x is defined as the ratio of the length of the adjacent side to the hypotenuse in a right-angled triangle with an angle of x radians.

FIGURE 6.3

$$\text{COS } x = \frac{A}{H}$$

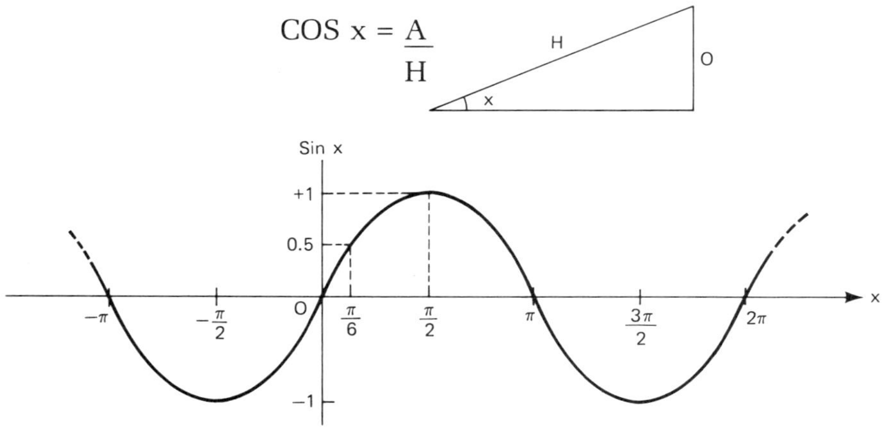

ARCCOS y [F] 

ARCCOS y is the angle whose COS is y.

TAN x [F] 

TAN x is defined as the ratio of the lengths of the opposite side to the adjacent side in a right-angled triangle with an angle of x radians.

FIGURE 6.4

$$\text{TAN } x = \frac{O}{A}$$

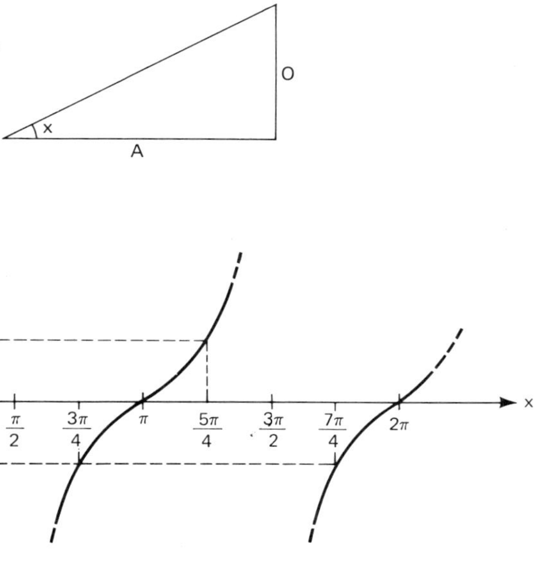

ARCTAN y [F] 

ARCTAN y is the angle whose TAN is y.
It can be proved mathematically that for any angle x,

$$SIN^2 (x) + COS^2 (x) = 1.$$

Program 9 illustrates this by allowing any angle to be entered and then calculates the SIN, the COS, and finally (SIN * SIN + COS * COS).

Program 9—SIN * SIN + COS * COS

```
 5 CLS
10 INPUT A
15 PRINT "ANGLE = ";A
20 LET S = SIN A
25 LET C = COS A
30 LET R = S * S + C * C
35 PRINT "S = "; S
40 PRINT "C = "; C
45 PRINT "S * S + C * C = "; R
50 INPUT Q$
55 IF Q$ = "" THEN GOTO 5
```

To enter another angle press NEWLINE first.

To return to command mode enter any character and then press NEWLINE.

The ZX81 has five more mathematical functions.

SQR (square root) [F] 

$$\text{SQR } x = \begin{cases} \sqrt{x} & \text{if } x >= 0 \\ \text{error} & x < 0 \end{cases}$$

ABS (absolute value) [F] 

$$\text{ABS } x = \begin{cases} x & \text{if } x >= 0 \\ -x & \text{if } x < 0 \end{cases}$$

SGN (signum) [F] 

$$\text{SGN } x = \begin{cases} +1 & \text{if } x > 0 \\ 0 & \text{if } x = 0 \\ -1 & \text{if } x < 0 \end{cases}$$

EXP (exponential) [F] 

$$\text{EXP } x = e^x$$

where e is defined as 2.718281828.

LN (natural logrithm) [F] 

$$\text{LN } x = \begin{cases} \log_e (x) & \text{if } x > 0 \\ \text{error} & \text{if } x <= 0 \end{cases}$$

CHAPTER SEVEN

The ZX81 Character Set and String Functions

The ZX81 character set can be visualized as its own unique alphabet consisting of 256 items which include alphabetic and numeric characters, mathematical symbols, pixel graphics, keywords, and so on. Each item is distinguished by its own code number which is an integer from 0 to 255.

There are two functions available on the ZX81 for converting characters into their code numbers and converting code numbers into their characters.

CHR$ F 

When applied to a number in the range 0< = x< =255, it returns the single character whose code is that number. For example,

```
10 LET A$ = CHR$ (38)
```

assigns "A" to the string variable A$ because the code of "A" is 38.

CODE F 

When applied to a string, it returns the code of the first character in the string.

```
10 LET A = CODE "A"
15 LET A = CODE "ABCDEF"
```

Both statements assign the value of 38 to variable A.

```
200 PRINT "DO YOU WISH TO CONTINUE?"
205 INPUT Q$
210 IF CODE Q$ = 51 THEN STOP
215 . . . . .
```

This section of a program causes execution to stop if NO, N, or anything else beginning with N is entered.

Program 10 displays the complete ZX81 character set on the screen.

Program 10—Character Set

```
 5 PRINT "ZX81 CHARACTER SET" , , ,
10 FOR I = 0 TO 255
15 PRINT CHR$ I ;
20 NEXT I
```

The other ZX81 string functions are as follows.

LEN [F] [K]

When applied to a string, it returns the number of characters in the string. That is,

```
10 LET A = LEN "ZX81"
```

assigns a value of 4 to variable A.

VAL [F] [J]

When applied to a string, it returns a result of the characters in the string being evaluated as an algebraic expression:

```
10 LET A = VAL "2 + 5 * 3"
```

assigns a value of 17 to variable A.

STR$ [F] [Y]

When applied to a number, it returns the digits in the number as a string:

```
10 LET A$ = STR$ 1000
```

assigns the string "1000" to string variable A$.

0. space

1.
2.
3.
4.
5.
6.
7.
8.
9.
10.
11. "
12. £
13. $
14. :
15. ?
16. (
17.)
18. >
19. <
20. =
21. +
22. –
23. *
24. /
25. ;
26. ,
27. .
28. 0
29. 1
30. 2
31. 3
32. 4
33. 5
34. 6
35. 7
36. 8
37. 9
38. A
39. B
40. C
41. D
42. E
43. F
44. G
45. H
46. I
47. J
48. K
49. L
50. M
51. N
52. O
53. P
54. Q
55. R
56. S
57. T
58. U
59. V
60. W
61. X
62. Y
63. Z
64. RND
65. INKEY$
66. PI
67.–111. not used
112. cursor up
113. cursor down
114. cursor left
115. cursor right
116. GRAPHICS
117. EDIT
118. NEWLINE
119. RUBOUT
120. mode
121. FUNCTION
122.–125. not used
126. constant
127. cursor

128.
129.
130.
131.
132.
133.
134.
135.
136.
137.
138.
139. inverse "
140. inverse £
141. inverse $
142. inverse :
143. inverse ?
144. inverse (
145. inverse)
146. inverse >
147. inverse <
148. inverse =
149. inverse +
150. inverse –
151. inverse *
152. inverse /
153. inverse ;
154. inverse ,
155. inverse .
156. inverse 0
157. inverse 1
158. inverse 2
159. inverse 3
160. inverse 4
161. inverse 5
162. inverse 6
163. inverse 7
164. inverse 8
165. inverse 9
166. inverse A
167. inverse B
168. inverse C
169. inverse D
170. inverse E
171. inverse F
172. inverse G
173. inverse H
174. inverse I
175. inverse J
176. inverse K
177. inverse L
178. inverse M
179. inverse N
180. inverse O
181. inverse P
182. inverse Q
183. inverse R
184. inverse S
185. inverse T
186. inverse U
187. inverse V
188. inverse W
189. inverse X
190. inverse Y
191. inverse Z
192. ""
193. AT
194. TAB
195. not used
196. CODE
197. VAL
198. LEN
199. SIN
200. COS
201. TAN
202. ASN
203. ACS
204. ATN
205. LN
206. EXP
207. INT
208. SQR
209. SGN
210. ABS
211. PEEK
212. USR
213. STR$
214. CHR$
215. NOT
216. **
217. OR
218. AND
219. <=
220. >=
221. <>
222. THEN
223. TO
224. STEP
225. LPRINT
226. LLIST
227. STOP
228. SLOW
229. FAST
230. NEW
231. SCROLL
232. CONT
233. DIM
234. REM
235. FOR
236. GOTO
237. GOSUB
238. INPUT
239. LOAD
240. LIST
241. LET
242. PAUSE
243. NEXT
244. POKE
245. PRINT
246. PLOT
247. RUN
248. SAVE
249. RAND
250. IF
251. CLS
252. UNPLOT
253. CLEAR
254. RETURN
255. COPY

Program n illustrates the use of CODE and LEN.

A large department store has issued credit cards to many of its regular customers. Each card has a nine-digit account number printed on it. To avoid fraud the department store owners need a security checking system to have a certain amount of safeguard with, for example, telephone orders, in which customers just quote their account numbers and the goods are dispatched.

The program enables the digits of the dubious account number to be entered; the computer will respond if the account number is invalid.

Program 11—Credit Cards

```
 5 INPUT A$
10 IF LEN A$<>9 THEN GOTO 5
15 PRINT A$
20 LET T = 0
25 FOR I = 1 TO 8
30 LET T = T + CODE A$ -28
35 LET A$ = A$(2 TO LEN A$)
40 NEXT I
45 IF T-10 * INT(T/10)<>CODE A$-28
      THEN PRINT "***** CARD INVALID *****"
```

The system is that the first eight digits of the account number are added together to produce a two-digit number. The second of these two digits is used as the ninth digit in the account number. For example,

Valid account number	7 8 7 7 5 4 3 6 7 Digits add up to 4<u>7</u>

line 10. This checks the length of A$ is 9. If it is not control jumps back to INPUT A$ again.

line 30. CODE A$–28 returns the first digit of A$ as a number and then adds it to T.

line 35. This assigns A$ without the first character back into A$. Some other computers including the 4K ROM, ZX80 have a function TL$ that removes the first character from a string.

line 45. Checks the second digit of the total is the same as the ninth digit of the account number.

CHAPTER EIGHT

Painting by Numbers

CONTROLLED PRINTING

We have already seen that information may be output on the screen by the PRINT statement followed by the list of items to be displayed separated by either a comma or a semicolon. There are two other methods for controlling the position on the screen where the information is to be printed.

TAB c [F] 

This moves the PRINT position to column c but if this involves back-spacing it will move onto the next line. If c is greater than 32 then the PRINT column will be the remainder when c is divided by 32.

AT 1,c [F] 

This moves the PRINT position to line 1 and column c where 0 < = 1 < = 21 and 0 < = c < = 31. For example,

```
10 PRINT TAB 10 ; "TOP"; AT 21,10 ; "BOTTOM";
         AT 10,0 ; "LEFT" ; TAB 10 ; "CENTRE";
         TAB 25 ; "RIGHT"
```

causes strings to be printed on the screen in their corresponding positions.

Program 12 demonstrates the use of PRINT AT.

Program 12—Poker Dice

```
  5 RAND
 10 PRINT AT 8,10; "1□2□3□4□5"
 15 FOR I = 1 TO 5
 20 GOSUB 100
 25 NEXT I
 30 FOR J = 1 TO 2
 35 INPUT R$
 40 IF R$ = "" THEN GOTO 65
 45 LET I = CODE R$ - 28
 50 GOSUB 100
 55 LET R$ = R$ (2 TO LEN R$)
 60 GOTO 40
 65 NEXT J
 70 PRINT AT 20,0; "PRESS N/L TO PLAY AGAIN"
 75 INPUT R$
 80 CLS
 85 IF R$ = "" THEN GOTO 10
 90 STOP
100 PRINT AT 10,8 + 2 * I; "9TJQKA"(INT(RND * 6 + 1))
105 RETURN
```

The program simulates a game of poker dice. There are five dice. On each die there is a 9, a 10 (T), a Jack (J), a Queen (Q), a King (K), and an Ace (A). Briefly the rules of the game are to obtain the highest hand given the following order:

Highest hand:	5 of the same
	4 of the same
	Run A K Q J T
	Run K Q J T 9
	3 of the same and 2 of the same
	3 of the same
	2 pairs
	1 pair
Lowest hand:	Ace high.

If two hands are the same, then the highest combination wins: 4 Aces beats 4 Tens, or a pair of Kings beats a pair of Queens.

The five dice are rolled and then the player is given an option twice of rethrowing any of the dice. A string is entered containing the numbers of the dice which are required to be rethrown: "24" would mean rethrow die 2 and die 4. After the second rethrow press NEWLINE to play again. To return to command mode press any character followed by NEWLINE.

The program works by printing the values of the die on line 10 of the screen in the columns 10, 12, 14, 16, and 18. When a die is rethrown, its new value is printed on top of its old value. A subroutine is used to roll the die and prints a single random character from the string "9TJQKA" in the correct position.

PLOTTING

Two other useful statements on the ZX81 are as follows.

PLOT x, y [K] 

This will black in a square with coordinates (x, y).

UNPLOT x, y [K] 

This will blank out a square with coordinates (x, y).

Figure 8.1 shows the coordinate positions on the display screen.

FIGURE 8.1

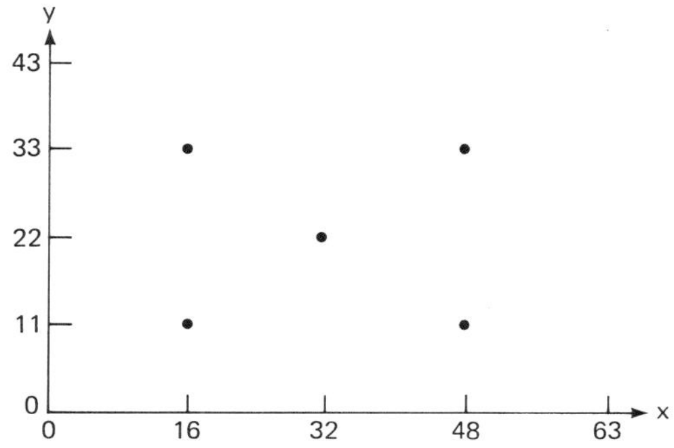

The next few examples illustrate how to use these commands for plotting curves.

1. *Circles.* The coordinates of the points on a circle are given by (a Cos Θ, a Sin Θ), where a is the radius of the circle.

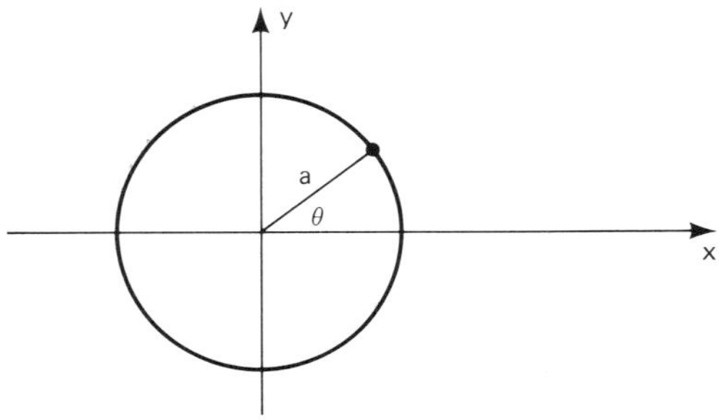

If we let Θ change from 0 to 2π we obtain points on the circle.

Program 13—Circle

```
 5 FOR I = 0 TO 2 * PI STEP PI/10
10 PLOT 30 + 10 * COS I, 22 + 10 * SIN I
15 NEXT I
20 PRINT AT 10,12; "CIRCLE"
```

Program 13 draws a circle of radius 10 units with its center at (30,22).

2. *Ellipses.* The coordinates of the points on an ellipse are given by (a Cos Θ, b Sin Θ).

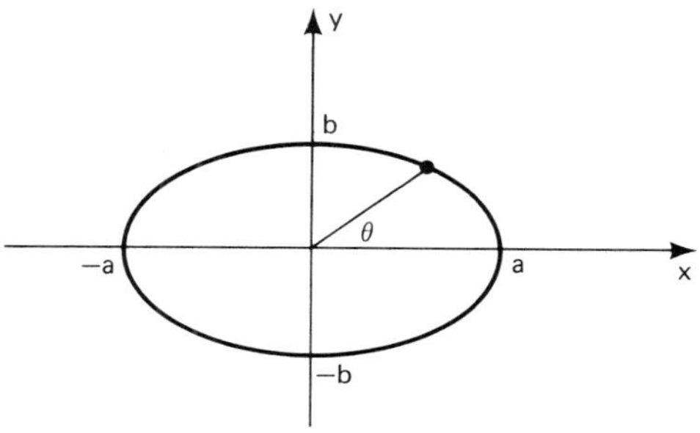

If we let Θ change from 0 to 2π, we obtain points on the ellipse.

Program 14—Ellipse

```
 5 FOR I = 0 TO 2 * PI STEP PI/10
10 PLOT 30 + 20 * COS I, 22 + 10 * SIN I
15 NEXT I
20 PRINT AT 10,12; "ELLIPSE"
```

This draws an ellipse with its center at (30,22).
3. *Sine wave.*

Program 15—Sine Wave

```
 5 FOR I = 0 TO 6 * PI STEP PI/10
10 PLOT I * 10/PI, 20 + 20 * SIN I
15 NEXT I
```

This draws a sine wave.

4. *Epicyclics.*

Program 16—Epicyclic

```
 5 FOR I = 0 TO 6 * PI STEP PI/20
10 PLOT 30 + 20 * COS (I * 2/3) * COS I,
        22 + 20 * COS (I * 2/3) * SIN I
15 NEXT I
```

This will draw a curve from the family of curves known as epicyclics. Try experimenting by changing the argument in COS(I * 2/3) to other values, for example, COS (I * 4/3).

PROGRAM 16 Epicyclics

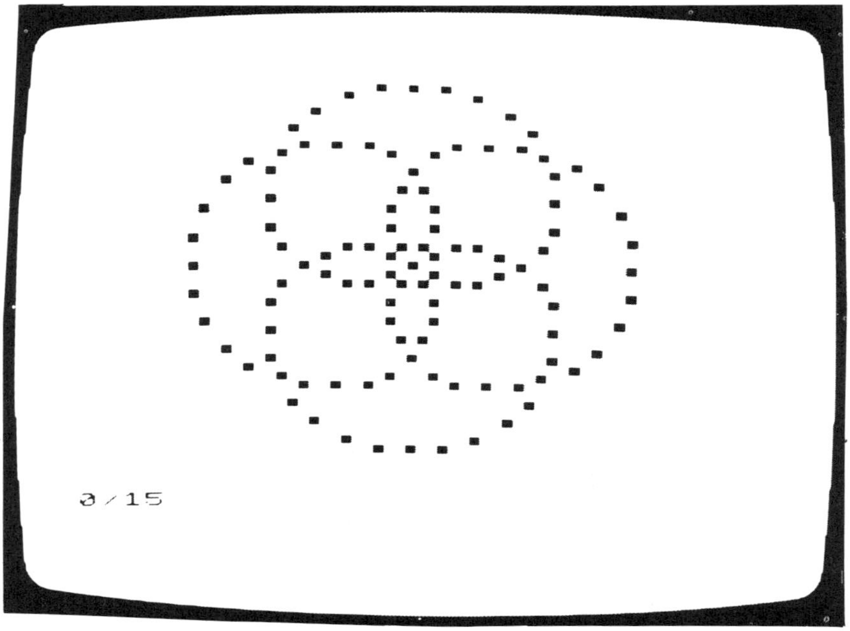

Program 17—Paper Doyleys

```
 5 FOR J = 2 TO 14 STEP 1
10 FOR I = 0 TO 2 * PI STEP PI/10
15 PLOT 30 + J * COS I, 22 + J * SIN I
20 NEXT I
25 NEXT J
```

This draws several circles of different radii giving interesting patterns. Try changing line 5 to STEP 2.

PROGRAM 17 Paper Doyleys

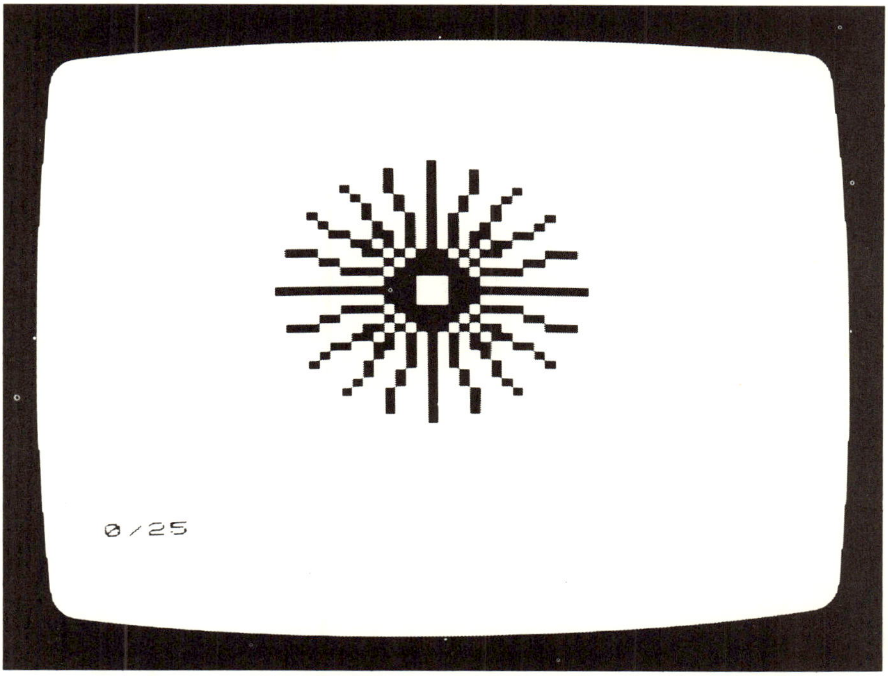

DRAWING GRAPHS

Program 18 shows one of the many ways of drawing a histogram graph for 12 items of numerical data, all of which are greater than or equal to zero. The main problem is for the computer to choose a suitable scale for the data. The method used in this case is to draw a line 25 units long for the largest item of data and draw the other lines in proportion. Each item of data is stored in the array D(12). If more or fewer items of data are required, lines 5, 15, and 35 must be modified by altering the 12 to the number of items. The maximum number is 22 since there are only 22 lines on the screen. The value of the data is also displayed on the screen but there is only sufficient space to display four digits. If more are required, then the argument for the TAB function in line 40 will have to be altered.

Program 18—Histogram

```
 5 DIM D (12)
10 LET MAX = 0
15 FOR I = 1 TO 12
20 INPUT D (I)
25 IF D (I) > MAX THEN LET MAX = D (I)
30 NEXT I
35 FOR I = 1 TO 12
40 PRINT D (I); TAB 4; "▐";
45 FOR J = 0.01 TO D (I) STEP MAX/25
50 PRINT "▒";
55 NEXT J
60 PRINT
65 NEXT I
```

PROGRAM 18 Histogram

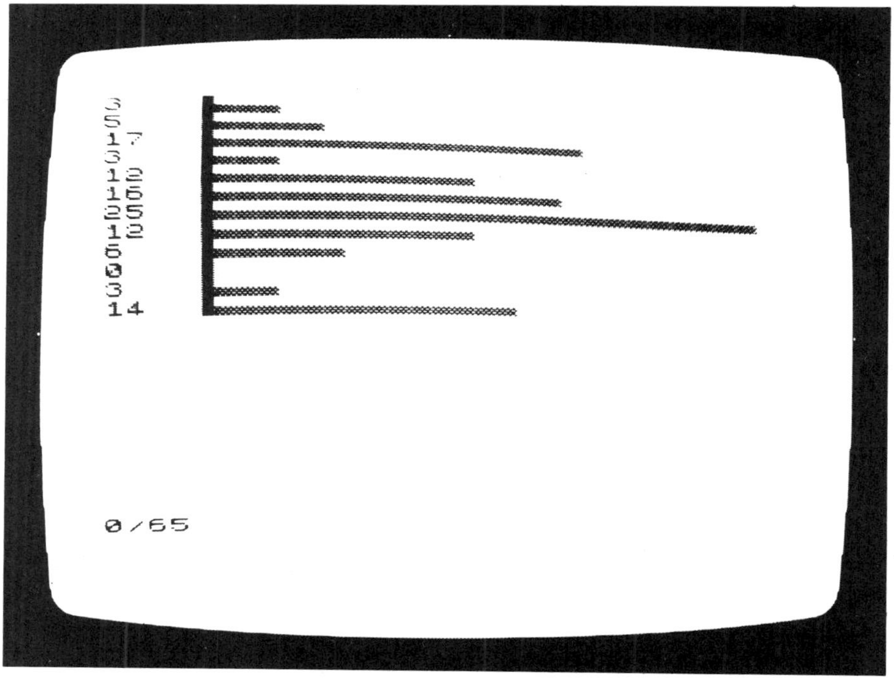

CHAPTER NINE

Speaking Logically

There are three logical operators :–

1. AND K or L [SHIFT] [2 AND] sometimes symbolized ^
2. OR K or L [SHIFT] [W UNPLOT OR COS] sometimes symbolized ˅
3. NOT F [N NEXT NOT] sometimes symbolized ¬

The AND and the OR are used between conditional statements as shown in Figure 9.1.

(condition 1) AND (condition 2) — AND gives a result *true* if and only if both operands are *true*. Otherwise the result is *false*.

(condition 1) OR (condition 2) — OR gives a result *false* if and only if both operands are *false*. Otherwise the result is *true*.

FIGURE 9.1

AND ∧	TRUE	FALSE
TRUE	TRUE	FALSE
FALSE	FALSE	FALSE

AND

FIGURE 9.2

OR ∨	TRUE	FALSE
TRUE	TRUE	TRUE
FALSE	TRUE	FALSE

OR

The NOT operator is used before a conditional statement.

NOT	(condition 1)	NOT gives a result *true* if the operand is *false* and a result *false* if the operand is *true*.

FIGURE 9.3

¬	
TRUE	FALSE
FALSE	TRUE

NOT

Logical operators are most frequently used in IF statements.

```
IF (A > B AND A > 5) OR (A < B AND A > 0) THEN statement
```

This "statement" would be executed if either

A is greater than B and A is greater than 5

or

A is less than B but A is greater than 0

Just as for numerical operators, logical operators are processed in a fixed order and not just simply from left to right. This is shown in Figure 9.4.

FIGURE 9.4

OPERATOR	PRIORITY
NOT	4
AND	3
OR	2

The NOTs are performed first, then the ANDs, and finally the ORs.

The computer does not actually recognize the logical values as "true" and "false" but as 1 (true) and 0 (false). In fact, any value other than 0 is recognized as true.

=, <, <=, >, >= and <> are numerical operators with a priority of 5.

```
10 LET A = B > C
```

assigns a value of

1 if B > C is true
0 if B > C is false

AND, OR, NOT are also numerical operators giving the following results.

1. A AND B returns a value A unless B is equal to zero in which case it returns a value 0.

$$\text{A AND B} = \begin{cases} \text{A if B not equal to 0} \\ \text{0 if B = 0} \end{cases}$$

2. A OR B returns a value 1 unless B is equal to zero in which case it returns a value A.

$$\text{A OR B} = \begin{cases} \text{1 if B not equal to 0} \\ \text{A if B = 0} \end{cases}$$

3. NOT A returns a value of 0 unless A is equal to zero in which case it returns a value 1.

$$\text{NOT A} = \begin{cases} \text{0 if A not equal to 0} \\ \text{1 if A = 0} \end{cases}$$

4. A$ AND B returns A$ unless B is equal to zero in which case it returns the empty string.

$$\text{A\$ AND B} = \begin{cases} \text{A\$ if B not equal to 0} \\ \text{“” if B = 0} \end{cases}$$

The following examples use the information in this chapter.

1. Test for an odd or even number.

```
10 IF N - 2 * INT (N/2) THEN PRINT " ODD"
```

An even number in the expression after the IF statement would give a value of 0, and so the PRINT statement would not be executed.

2. GOTO statements.

```
10 GOTO (100 AND A = 5) + (120 AND A < 5)
                        + (140 AND A > 5)
```

If A = 5 control will go to line 100. If A < 5 control will go to line 120. If A > 5 control will go to line 140.

3. Max.-Min.

It is possible to assign either the maximum or minimum of two numbers to a variable.

```
10 INPUT A
15 INPUT B
20 LET MAX = (A AND A >= B) + (B AND A < B)
25 LET MIN = (A AND A <= B) + (B AND A > B)
30 PRINT "MAXIMUM "; MAX
35 PRINT "MINIMUM "; MIN
40 GOTO 10
```

4. Strings.

```
50 LET A$ = ("YES" AND A >= 0)
          + ("NO" AND A < 0)
```

This assigns the string "YES" if A is greater than or equal to 0, or "NO" if A is less than 0, to the string variable A$.

CHAPTER TEN

Using INKEY$

INKEY$ [F] [B]

An excellent feature of the ZX81 is its ability to sense what key is being pressed during the execution of a program. The function INKEY$ is used but with no argument. If control comes across INKEY$ when a program is being executed, INKEY$ returns whatever character the key in [L] mode represents. The pressing of SHIFT and one other key is valid. If no key is being pressed the empty string "" is returned. The input of information using INKEY$ has the advantage over INPUT that it does not have to be followed by NEWLINE.

To input information using INKEY$ a loop may be set up so that if no key is being pressed the empty string is recognized and control does not proceed. If a key is then pressed, control continues and the value of INKEY$ can be assigned to a string variable. For example,

```
 5 IF INKEY$ = "" THEN GOTO 5
10 LET A$ = INKEY$
```

An important note is that INKEY$ could possibly change between lines. It is advisable that, as soon as INKEY$ returns a feasible value, it be stored in a string variable and that variable, rather than INKEY$, then be used.

This idea is used in Program 19. This program can be used for writing a letter on the screen and if the printer is attached a printed copy can be obtained.

Program 19—Word Processor

```
 5 IF INKEY$<> "" THEN GOTO 5
10 IF INKEY$ = "" THEN GOTO 10
15 LET A$ = INKEY$
20 IF CODE A$ = 113 THEN GOTO 50
25 IF CODE A$ = 114 THEN CLS
30 IF CODE A$ = 115 THEN PRINT
35 IF CODE A$ = 118 THEN PRINT "□";
40 IF CODE A$ < 112 OR CODE A$ > 118 THEN PRINT A$;
45 GOTO 5
50 COPY
```

8K ROM ZX80 modification: Replace lines 5 & 10 with

```
5 PAUSE 40000
```

If any key is touched, the corresponding character will be displayed on the screen. Characters that are normally accessed by using the SHIFT key may also be used.

Because the space key is also BREAK we have to use a different key to display a space. The program uses the NEWLINE key to represent a space. There are also three other keys that have special meanings. ⇩ causes the printing to start on the next line, ⇧ causes the screen to be cleared and ⇦ causes a copy of the screen to be sent to the printer.

Without any memory expansion the screen is limited to about 18 lines. Line 5 enables the computer to know that you have taken your finger off a key. If this line is not included, when a key is pressed the corresponding character will be continually printed for as long as the key is pressed.

The program can be modified so that when a COPY is called for, it will also print out the address at the top and the name at the bottom.

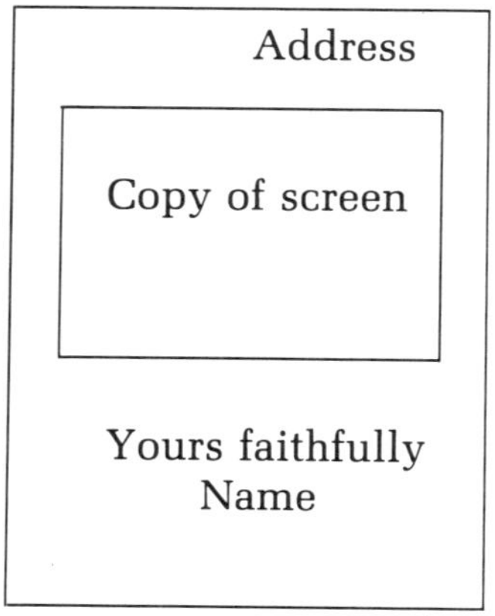

Program 20—Sketcher I

```
 5 LET X = 30
10 LET Y = 20
15 IF INKEY$ = "" THEN GOTO 15
20 LET A$ = INKEY$
25 IF Y < 43 AND (A$ = "E" OR A$ = "W" OR A$ = "Q")
          THEN LET Y = Y + 1
30 IF Y > 0 AND (A$ = "Z" OR A$ = "X" OR A$ = "C")
          THEN LET Y = Y - 1
35 IF X < 63 AND (A$ = "E" OR A$ = "D" OR A$ = "C")
          THEN LET X = X + 1
40 IF Y > 0 AND (A$ = "Q" OR A$ = "A" OR A$ = "Z")
          THEN LET X = X - 1
45 IF A$ = "S" THEN CLS
50 PLOT X, Y
55 GOTO 15
```

8K ROM ZX80 modification: Replace line 15 with

```
15 PAUSE 40000
```

This program plots a line in one of eight desired directions. It is possible to change this direction as many times as required, thus producing a picture. The direction required is obtained by pressing the corresponding key in the diagram in Figure 10.1.

FIGURE 10.1

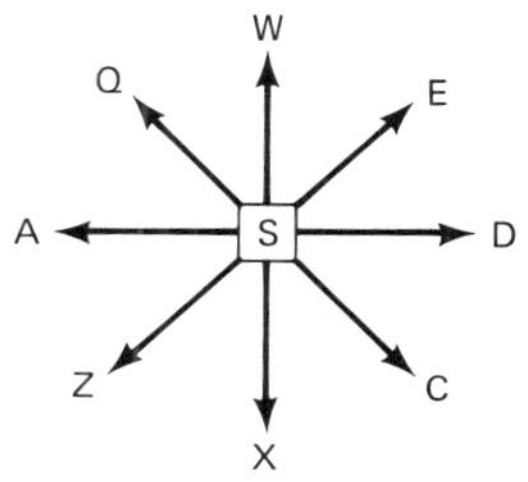

"S" clears the screen. To stop the program press the BREAK key.

Without the memory expansion, the display is liable to fill up if the right-hand side of the screen is used and this will cease the execution of the program. The solution is to try and draw toward the left-hand side of the screen; the reason for this is explained in Chapter 11.

The program works by storing the present coordinates of the point being plotted on the screen in variables X and Y. These are either increased or decreased by 1 depending on the required direction provided that X and Y are within the limits that PLOT will allow.

PROGRAM 20 Sketcher I

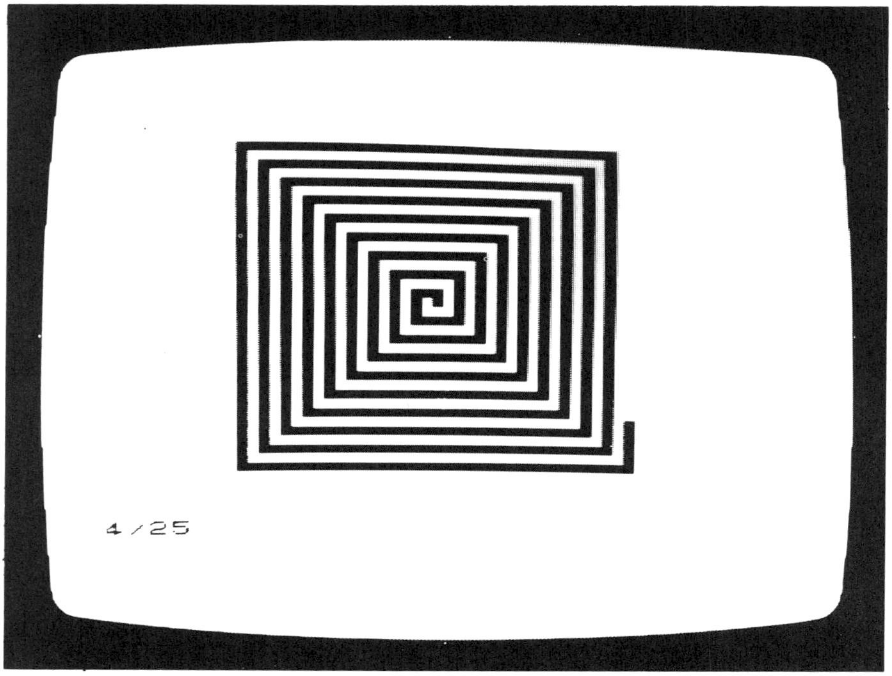

CHAPTER ELEVEN

The ZX81 Memory

The ZX81 memory, like that in any other computer, can be visualized as a long column of cells, each of which has an identification number called its address. The ZX81 memory is subdivided as shown in Figures 11.1 and 11.2.

The first 8192 bytes contain the software that operates the computer. This memory is ROM (Read Only Memory).

The standard ZX81 has 1024 bytes available for the user situated from address 16384 to 17407. When the 16K memory expansion is attached, the user memory consists of 16384 bytes situated from address 16384 to 32767. The user memory is RAM (Random Access Memory).

SYSTEM VARIABLES

Figure 11.2 shows how the user memory is subdivided. The area of system variables at the top of the RAM contains several pieces of information for specific uses by the computer which, for example, include items such as a seed for random number generation, position on line where the next character is to be printed, address of each of the boundaries between the various sections in the RAM shown in Figure 11.2, and so on.

Each of the system variables has a name; VARS, for example, is the name of the system variable which contains the address of the section storing the variables. This name however has nothing to do with a BASIC variable VARS.

The complete set of system variables is covered comprehensively in Chapter 28 of the ZX81 operating manual.

FIGURE 11.1 ZX81 Memory Layout

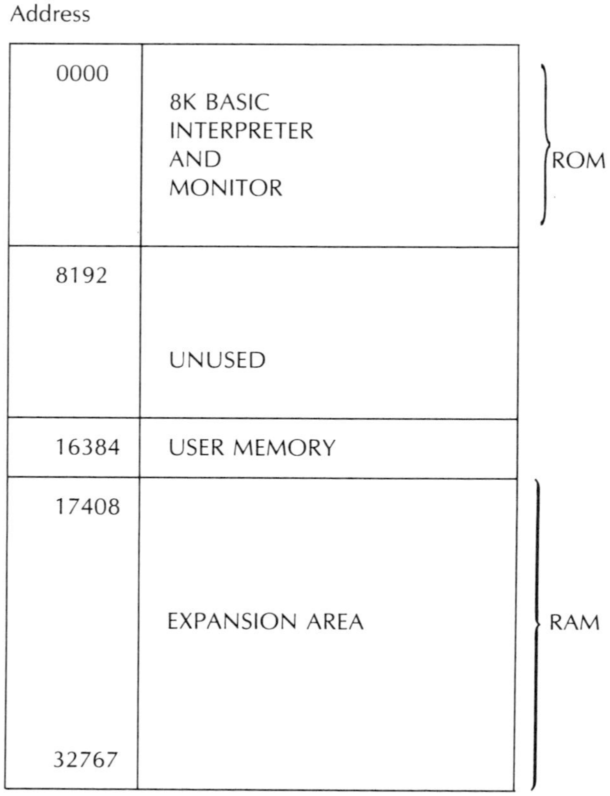

FIGURE 11.2 ZX81 RAM Layout

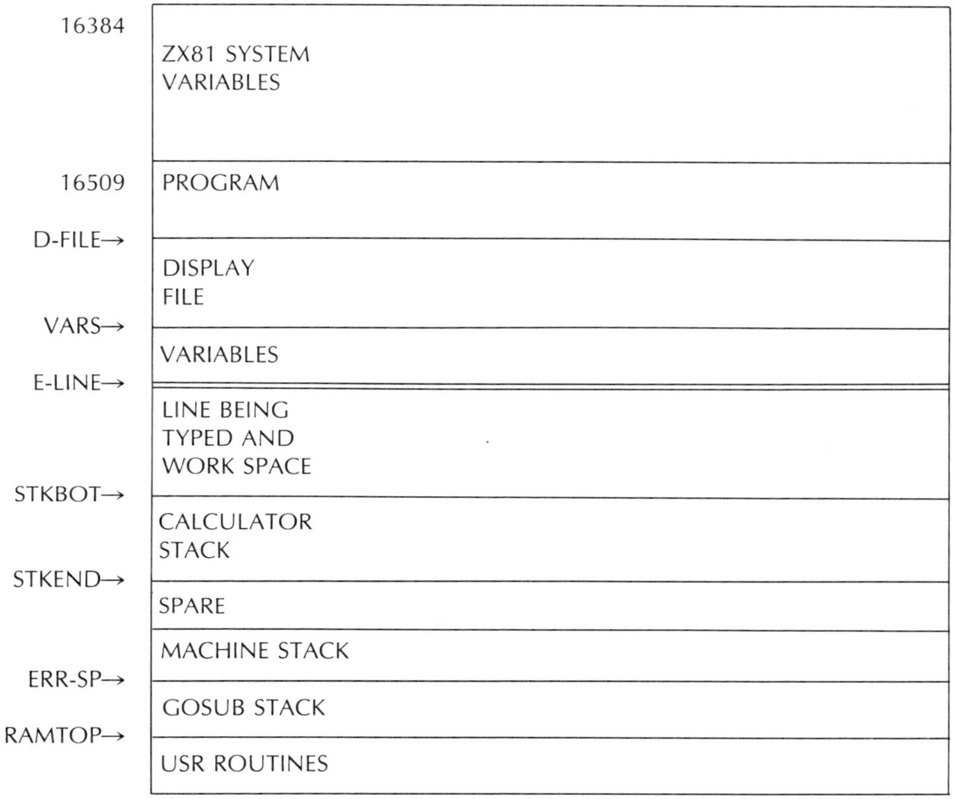

PROGRAM FILE

The user program is situated between addresses 16509 and D-FILE. Each line of the program is stored in the form shown in Figure 11.3

FIGURE 11.3

Line Number	Length of Text + 1	.... Program Text	NEWLINE
2 bytes	2 bytes		1 byte

We shall later use this information to write a program that will renumber the lines in another program in steps of 5.

If a line is entered into the program file, all the contents in the RAM from the address where the line is stored will be shifted up in memory. Likewise, if a program line is deleted, all the contents will be shifted down in memory.

DISPLAY FILE

The display file contains the information that is displayed on the screen. It is situated between addressed D-FILE and VARS.

The display file starts with 25 NEWLINEs. Each of the possible 24 lines on the screen is stored between the corresponding NEWLINEs. This method enables lines on the screen consisting of fewer than 32 characters not to have to occupy 32 bytes (see Figure 11.4).

FIGURE 11.4 Example of Display File Where Three Lines Are Displayed on the Screen

```
NEWLINE 1
<<line 1 . . . . . . . .>>NEWLINE 2
<<line 2 . . . . . . . . . . . .>>NEWLINE 3
<<line 3 . . . .>>NEWLINE 4
NEWLINE 5
NEWLINE 6
≡
NEWLINE 25
```

However when memory is plentiful (greater than 3¼K), 32 spaces are always stored before each NEWLINE.

VARIABLES

All the variables are stored between addresses VARS and E-LINE.

The method of storage depends on the type of variable. The name of the variable is stored by the CODE of its characters in the name, plus a certain number which is used to distinguish the different types of variables.

1. Single character numerical variable (Figure 11.5).

FIGURE 11.5

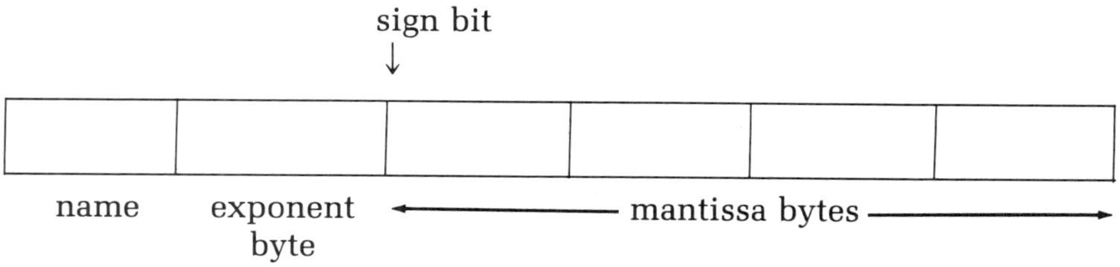

The name is stored as the CODE of the name of the variable + 64.

The exponent byte lies between 1 and 255 and is used to indicate the position of the decimal point.

The four mantissa bytes give the digits of the number. These bytes give a number between ½ and 1.

The actual number is obtained by

```
m*2** (e-128)
```

where m is the mantissa bytes and e is the exponent byte.

The first bit stored in the mantissa bytes is set with 0 if the number is positive and 1 if the number is negative.

2. Multiple character numerical variable (Figure 11.6).

FIGURE 11.6

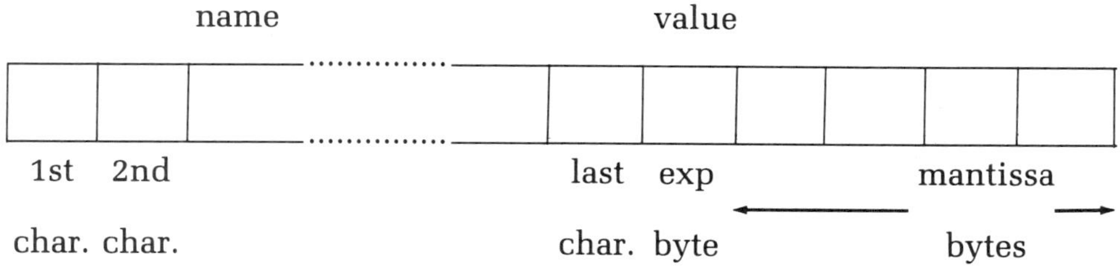

The first and last characters in the name are distinguished because they are stored by their CODE + 128. All the other characters are stored just by their CODE.

3. Numerical array (Figure 11.7)

FIGURE 11.7

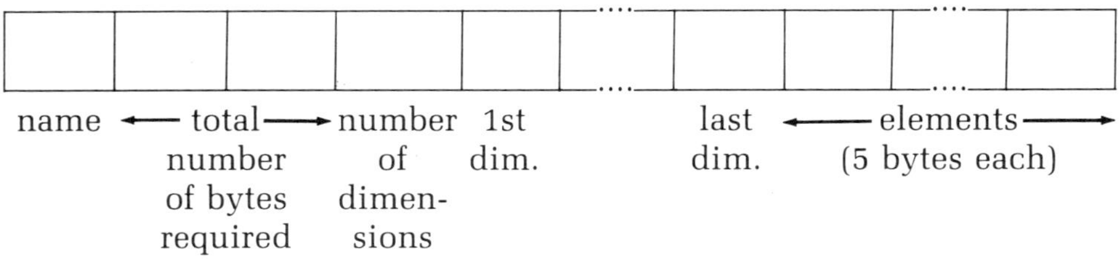

A numerical array is recognized by storing the name by its CODE + 96.

The elements are stored in an order such that first come those whose first subscript is 1, then 2, and so on up to its maximum first subscript. Each section with the same first subscript is then ordered so that the second subscripts are in increasing order. This continues for all the subscripts. Consider the array A(2,2,2); the elements are stored in the order:

```
A(1,1,1)
A(1,1,2)
A(1,2,1)
A(1,2,2)
A(2,1,1)
A(2,1,2)
A(2,2,1)
A(2,2,2)
```

4. Control variable (Figure 11.8).

FIGURE 11.8

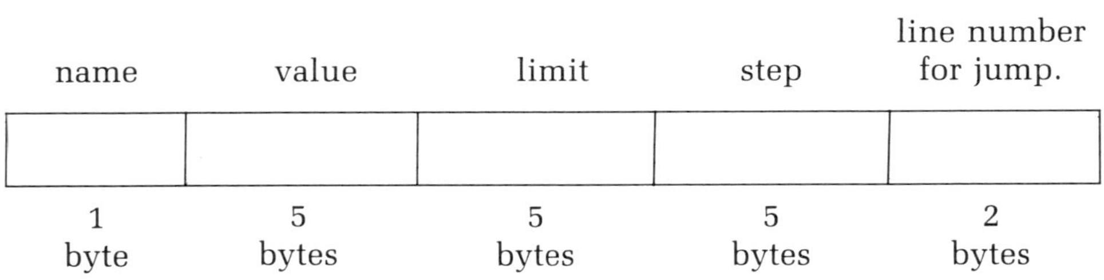

A control variable is recognized by storing the name by its CODE + 192.

The control variable also stores the line number of the FOR statement that defined it plus 1. This is so that control knows where to jump to when NEXT is executed.

GOSUB STACK

The GOSUB stack is used to tell control which line to continue from after a RETURN statement is executed.

A stack is a method of storing and retrieving data in a computer; most recent item of data stored will be the first retrieved. Storing information is known as *pushing* onto the stack and retrieving information is known as *popping* the stack (Figure 11.9).

FIGURE 11.9

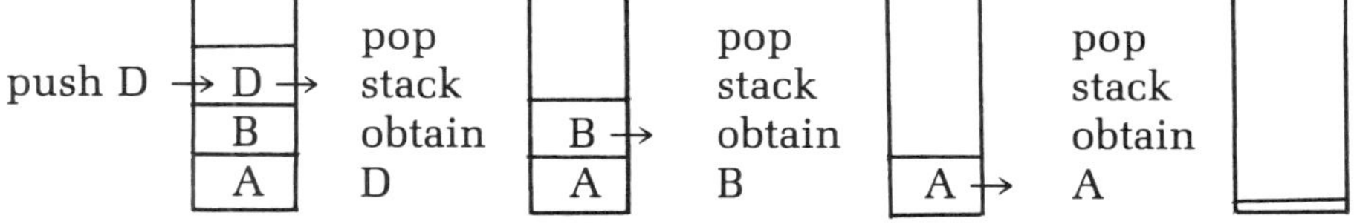

The ZX81 uses a stack like this to deal with GOSUB. When control executes GOSUB n, the line number +1 of the statement is pushed onto the stack and control continues from line n. When control executes a RETURN, it continues from the line number which is popped from the stack. If a RETURN is executed before any GOSUB statement, an empty stack will be popped and this will cause an error to be displayed.

THE 16K RAM PACK

The ZX81 has 1K of internal RAM but since a large section of this is required to store the system variables, the display file, and the variables, you will probably soon find that the remaining memory is inadequate for writing interesting programs.

A 16K RAM pack is available which replaces the internal 1K memory by slotting onto the expansion port situated at the rear of the ZX81. The same 16K RAM pack used on a ZX80 may also be used on a ZX81. It is important that, when the RAM pack is either slotted on or off the ZX81, the power supply be disconnected or some damage to the unit may be caused.

The only noticeable difference with the RAM pack connected is that when the power is first switched on, the cursor takes a little longer to appear. This is because when the power is first switched on, the operating system checks to see how much RAM is available and with 16K this takes a little longer.

With the RAM pack, since the memory is plentiful, the display file does not work in its usual manner of only using as much memory as it needs (see Figure 11.4), but is always filled with 32 spaces on each of the 24 lines. One exception to this is when SCROLL is executed: this causes the empty bottom line that appears to be stored in the display file by the twenty-fourth and twenty-fifth NEWLINE characters to be together with no characters in between them.

If your RAM pack develops problems, as, for example, the contents of the memory decaying, check that the contacts of the expansion port are clean. Although the contacts in the RAM pack are gold plated, the contacts on the printed circuit board of the ZX81 are not gold and can become oxidized (a chemical reaction takes place between the air and the surface of the contact), leaving a deposit which causes a bad connection when the RAM pack is slotted on. Carefully clean the contacts with alcohol or acetone.

CHAPTER TWELVE

PEEKing and POKEing

There are two instructions in ZX81 BASIC which enable us to directly access memory cells in the computer. One is used to store data in a specific memory cell. The other is used to retrieve data. While these instructions may seem curious at first, understanding them comprehensively opens the way for increased computing power.

The first instruction is POKE [K] [0]. This statement enables an algebraic expression to be evaluated and the result stored in a specific address. The syntax of the statement is

line number POKE a, e

where e is the algebraic expression and a is the address in the memory.

```
10 POKE 16436, 255
```

This stores 255 at address 16436.

The second instruction is PEEK [F] [0]. This function returns the value of the byte at an address specified.

```
20 LET A = PEEK 16436
```

This assigns the value stored at address 16436 to A.

Addresses in both the ROM and the RAM may be PEEKed, but POKE is strictly limited to the RAM, that is, from address 16384 onward.

The following examples illustrate just a few of the numerous uses of PEEK and POKE.

TIMER

A television frame counter is contained in the addresses 16436 and 16437. This system variable is called FRAMES (Figure 12.1).

FIGURE 12.1

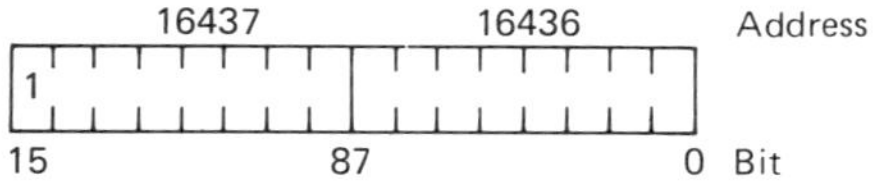

The television frame counter works by decrementing the value contained in bits 0 to 14 by one every time a frame is displayed on the screen. In the United States it is 60 times every second. Bit 15 is set to 1.

With this facility we have the scope to add timings to our programs for uses such as a stopwatch or for timing moves in games. To achieve this we first have to preset FRAMES with a known value. After a certain length of time, the contents of FRAMES can be PEEKed and by comparing with the initial value, we find the number of frames displayed. Dividing the number of frames by 60, yields the time in seconds.

```
 5 POKE 16437, 255
10 POKE 16436, 255
15 FOR I = 1 TO 10
20 LET A = (65535 - PEEK 16436 - 256 * PEEK 16437)/60
25 PRINT A
30 NEXT I
```

Lines 5 and 10 set each byte of FRAMES to 255. This sets each bit to 1. FRAMES now stores 65535.

Lines 15 to 30 is a FOR loop, and on each looping the time taken in seconds since the program was RUN is displayed.

Line 20 calculates how many frames have been displayed. When control executes PEEK 16436 + 256 * PEEK 16437, it returns the value of FRAMES at that particular instant. Subtracting this away from the initial value of 65535 gives the number of frames displayed, and dividing this by 60 gives the time in seconds.

Program 21—Reaction Timer

```
 5 RAND
10 FOR I = 0 TO RND STEP 0.005
15 CLS
20 NEXT I
25 POKE 16437, 255
30 POKE 16436, 255
35 PRINT AT 10, 12; "BANG"
40 IF INKEY$ <>"X" THEN GOTO 40
45 PRINT AT 14,4; "TIME TAKEN "; (65535  -
   PEEK 16436 - 256 * PEEK 16437 - 5)/ 60; " SECS"
50 IF INKEY$ <>"C" THEN GOTO 50
55 GOTO 10
```

This program will not run on an 8K ROM ZX80.

Program 21 uses the same principal described for timing, to test a person's reactions.

To use, execute the program with RUN. When "BANG" appears at the center of the screen, press key X and the time taken to react will be displayed.

To have another attempt press key C (Continue).

To stop press BREAK.

line 5	Sets sequence of random numbers to commence at an unknown position.
line 10–20	This loop is executed for a random time and so gives a delay for an unknown length of time.
line 25–30	Sets FRAMES to initial value.
line 35	Prints BANG on the screen.
line 40	Tests for X key.
line 45	Evaluates and prints time taken. Notice that 5/60 was subtracted. This is the delay time for the signal to reach the central processing unit and the time taken to execute line 35. If key X is pressed before BANG appears, a time of zero seconds should be obtained.
line 50	Tests for C key.

CALCULATING THE LENGTH OF A PROGRAM

By looking at Figure 11.2, it is seen that the program file commences at address 16509. The address of the end of the program file is stored as a system variable called D-FILE at addresses 16396/7.

The difference between the contents of D-FILE and 16509 is equal to the number of bytes in the program.

```
9999 PRINT "LENGTH OF PROGRAM ";
            PEEK 16396 + 256 * PEEK 16397 - 16509
```

Because line 9999 is not part of the program whose length is required we should subtract the number of bytes that line 9999 occupies. This is found by executing line 9999 without any other lines in the program. Line 9999 is found to occupy 74 bytes and so should be modified to

```
9999 PRINT "LENGTH OF PROGRAM ";
            PEEK 16396 + 256 * PEEK 16397 - 16583
```

This will give the length of a program but does not differentiate between the memory required for variables, the display file and so on. However, line 9999 is useful for comparing similar programs and for learning what program methods are more efficient with memory space.

To execute line 9999 and not the program whose length is required, press

```
RUN 9999    (NEWLINE)
```

POKEING CHARACTERS INTO THE DISPLAY FILE

Many interesting programs require a large display file, but this uses up valuable programming space. Sometimes the screen is required to be amended and an efficient method is needed that uses little programming space. There are three ways of effecting this.

1. The section of the screen can be altered by printing on top of it using PRINT AT.
2. The screen is cleared by CLS and the display rebuilt; this is done line by line which has to be stored and so uses up more memory.
3. The screen can be altered by POKEing characters into the display file. This technique has the advantage of being able to PEEK addresses in the display file and seeing what characters

are in certain positions. Another advantage over the rebuilding of the screen is that the amended picture is achieved much faster.

Program 22 illustrates this method.

Program 22—Sketcher II

```
 5 LET P = 210
10 LET A$ = "*"
15 FOR I = 1 TO 320
20 PRINT " . ";
25 NEXT I
30 POKE PEEK 16396 + PEEK 16397 * 256 + P,
                                     CODE A$
35 IF INKEY$ = "" THEN GOTO 35
40 LET B$ = INKEY$
45 LET P = P + (32 AND B$ = "Z")
             + (33 AND B$ = "X")
             + (34 AND B$ = "C")
             - (34 AND B$ = "Q")
             - (33 AND B$ = "W")
             - (32 AND B$ = "E")
             + ( 1 AND B$ = "D")
             - ( 1 AND B$ = "A")
50 IF B$ = "S" THEN INPUT A$
55 GOTO 30
```

8K ROM ZX80 Modification. Change line 35 to

```
PAUSE 40000
```

Sketcher II enables a picture to be drawn on the screen.

FIGURE 12.2

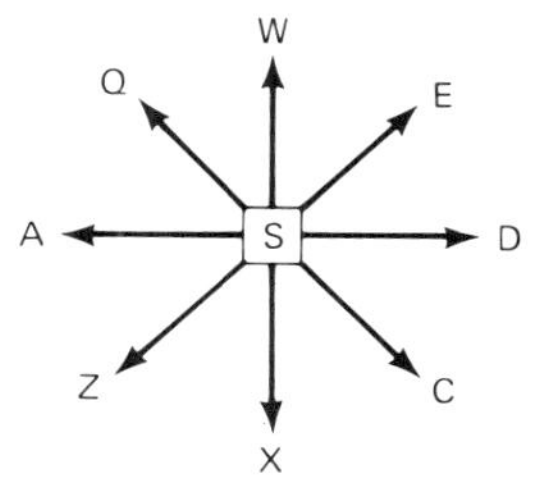

To move the character on the screen, press the key corresponding to the desired direction as shown in Figure 12.2.

To change the character, press the S key, then the required character and finally NEWLINE.

It is very important not to let the line being drawn leave the edge of the screen or a character will be POKEd in a position not in the display file. This could produce some undesirable results such as changing the information in the program file.

Variable P is the position from the top of the display file where the character is to be POKEd and string variable A$ is the character.

Lines 15–25 set up the display file with 10 lines. If the memory expansion is connected, this can be increased to 22 lines. The starting address of the display file is stored at 16396/7 (D-FILE) in the system variables and so line 35 POKEs the character into an address P places from the top of the display file. Line 45 modifies P so that the character will be POKEd into another position. Figure 12.3 shows how much P must be altered for the required directions.

FIGURE 12.3

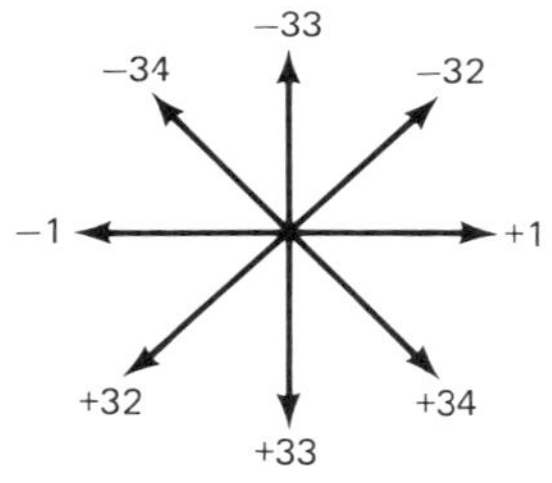

Another useful system variable is DF-CC address 16398/9 which contains the address in the display file of the PRINT position.

ENLARGED CHARACTERS

The 8K ROM in the ZX81 holds a character generator from address 7688 to address 8191. The character generator contains information on what the character looks like. The binary representation of every eight bytes contains the formation pattern of each character:

```
THE CHARACTER "$ "
```

FIGURE 12.4

ADDRESS	NUMBER	BINARY
7784	0	00000000
7785	8	00001000
7786	62	00111110
7787	40	00101000
7788	62	00111110
7789	10	00001010
7790	62	00111110
7791	8	00001000

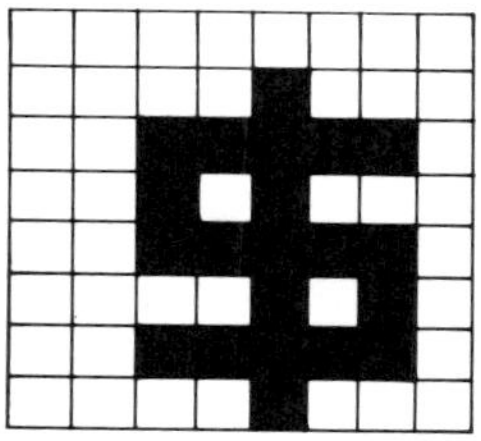

Program 23 displays all the characters on the ZX81 eight times larger than normal.

Program 23—Enlarged Characters

```
 5 FOR J = 7688 TO 8191
10 LET A = PEEK J
15 FOR I = 7 TO 0 STEP -1
20 PRINT AT 20, I; CHRS$ ((A-2* INT(A/2)) * 128)
25 LET A = INT(A/2)
30 NEXT 1
35 PRINT AT 20,10; J
40 SCROLL
45 NEXT J
```

Each byte in the character generator is taken in turn and its binary form is printed out using a ■ for 1 and a □ for 0.
8K ROM ZX80 Modification. Add line 42

```
PAUSE 30
```

MACHINE CODE PROGRAMMING

This book is not really intended to teach the writing of machine code programs but to show the ZX81 user how to execute and possibly understand other people's machine code programs.

What is machine code?

As mentioned earlier a computer cannot directly process a high-level language such as BASIC, but has to convert it into a simpler form that it can understand, called *machine code.*

A machine code program may be displayed as a list of pairs of hexadecimal digits. Each pair is a code for a certain instruction that the computer will execute.

There are two different methods used by computers to convert the program into a machine code form:

i. *Using a compiler* Before the program is executed, the compiler is used to translate the program into a machine code program. This machine code program can then be executed as many times as required.

ii. *Using an interpreter* The program is executed and as control reaches each statement, it is converted by the interpreter into a machine code form that the computer can understand.

The ZX81 uses a BASIC interpreter, which is a section of software contained in the 8K ROM.

Why use machine code?

It is possible on the ZX81 to execute a machine code program directly and not bother to use the BASIC interpreter. There are two advantages in doing this:

i. Machine code programs use less memory space than equivalent high-level language programs.

ii. Machine code programs are executed much faster than equivalent high-level language programs. The quick execution of programs is vital for such uses as fast action games or complex games like chess, when a response is required within a reasonable time. When an interpreter is used, if a certain statement is executed several times the conversion into its machine code form has to be repeated each time, and this is time consuming.

The Z80 central processing unit

The ZX81 (and ZX80) use the Z80 or the NBL 780-1 equivalent central processing unit. The Z80 CPU contains eighteen 8-bit registers and four 16-bit registers which are used to store information. These include two sets of six general-purpose, 8-bit registers which may also be used in pairs as 16-bit registers. One set of these registers is called BC, DE, and HL, and the other set is called B'C', D'E', and H'L'. There are two sets of accumulator and flag registers. An accumulator holds the result of arithmetic and logical operations and its flag register is a group of 8 bits each indicating a specific condition on the result of arithmetic and logical operations. The remaining registers also have specific purposes in the executing of the program.

FIGURE 12.5 The Z80 General Purpose Registers

Accumulator	A	B	D	H	Main registers
Flag	F	C	E	L	
Accumulator	A'	B'	D'	H'	Alternative registers
Flag	F'	C'	E'	L'	

The Z80 instruction set

The instructions available on the Z80 CPU are shown in Figure 12.6. Most of the instructions are written as abbreviations known as mnemonics, for example, LD means Load which is the term used for storing data in a CPU register.

Instruction/Data (hex)	Mnemonic
06	LD B, n(n = 30h)
30	
0E	LD C, n(n = 25h)
25	
C9	RETURN

In this program, each instruction or data value which is a two-digit hexadecimal number occupies one 8-bit byte. The program loads the value of 30h (HBX) into register B and 25h into register C.

The same job could be done by loading BC as a 2-byte register.

Instruction/Data (hex)	Mnemonic
01	LD BC, nm(m = 25h)(n = 30h)
25	
30	
C9	RETURN

Note that the least significant byte is loaded first.

It is also possible to load the contents of one register into another.

```
78    LD A,B
```

will load the contents of B into the accumulator A. And we can add to the contents of the accumulator:

```
80    ADD A,B
```

will add the contents of B to the contents of the accumulator A. The result is stored in A while B remains unaltered.

Other operations carried out by the Z80 include subtraction, logical AND, logical OR, logical X OR, compare, shifting and rotating the bits in a register, incrementing or decrementing a register by 1, the manipulation of individual bits in a register, jumps, stack operations, and I/O operations.

One final comment about the codes is indirect addressing. Instructions using indirect addressing have brackets surrounding a 16-bit register pair in the abbrevations in Figure 12.6

```
LD A, (HL)
```

This does not mean Load the contents of HL into A, but Load the contents stored in the address specified by HL into A.

Anybody wishing to learn and understand the Z80 codes comprehensively should obtain a book specializing on the matter, among them, *Programming the Z80*, by R. Zaks, published by Sybex.

FIGURE 12.6 Z80 Mnemonics

Least Significant Byte

Most Significant Byt	0	1	2	3	4	5	6	7	8	9	A	B	C	D	E	F
0	NOP	LC BC, nn	LD (BC),A	INC BC	INC B	DEC B	LD B, n	ALCA	EX AF, AF'	ADD HL, BC	LD A, (BC)	DEC BC	INC C	DEC C	LD C, n	RRCA
1	DJNZ disp	LD DE, nn	LD (DE), A	INC DE	INC D	DEC D	LD D, n	RLA	JR disp	ADD HL, DE	LD A, (DE)	DEC DE	INC E	DEC E	LD E, n	RRA
2	JRNZ disp	LD HL, nn	LD (nn), HL	INC HL	INC H	DEC H	LD H, n	DAA	JRZ disp	ADD HL, HL	LD HL, (nn)	DEDC HL	INC L	DEC L	LD L, n	CPL
3	JR NC disp	LD SP, nn	LD (nn), A	INC SP	INC (HL)	DEC (HL)	LD (HL), n	SCF	JRC disp	ADD HL, sp	LD A, (nn)	DEC SP	INC A	DEC A	LD A, n	CCF
4	LD B, B	LD B, C	LD B, D	LD B, E	LD B, H	LD B, L	LD B, (HL)	LD B, A	LD C, B	LD C, C	LD C, D	LD C, E	LD C, H	LD C, L	LD C, (HL)	LD C, A
5	LD D, B	LD D, C	LD D, D	LD D, E	LD D, H	LD D, L	LD D, (HL)	LD D, A	LD E, B	LD E, C	LD E, D	LD E, E	LD E, H	LD E, L	LD E, (HL)	LD E, A
6	LD H, B	LD H, C	LD H, D	LD H, E	LD H, H	LD H, L	LD H, (HL)	LD H, A	LD L, B	LD L, C	LD L, D	LD L, E	LD L, H	LD L, L	LD L, (HL)	LD L, A
7	LD (HL), B	LD (HL), C	LD (HL), D	LD (HL), E	LD (HL), H	LD (HL), L	HALT	LD (HL),A	LD A, B	LD A, C	LD A, B	LD A, E	LD A, H	LD A, L	LD A, (HL)	LD A, A
8	ADD A, B	ADD A, C	ADD A, D	ADD A, E	ADD A, H	ADD A, L	ADD A, (HL)	ADD A, A	ADC A, B	ADC A, C	ADC A, D	ADC A, E	ADC A, H	ADC A, L	ACD A, (HL)	ADC A, A
9	SUB B	SUB C	SUB D	SUB E	SUB H	SUB L	SUB (HL)	SUB A	SBC A, B	SBC A, C	SBC A, D	SBC A, E	SBC A, H	SBC A, L	SBC A, (HL)	SBC A, A
A	AND B	AND C	AND D	AND E	AND H	AND L	AND (HL)	AND A	XOR B	XOR C	XOR D	XOR E	XOR H	XOR L	XOR (HL)	XOR A
B	OR B	OR C	OR D	OR E	OR H	OR L	OR (HL)	OR A	CP B	CP C	CP D	CP E	CP H	CP L	CP (HL)	CP A
C	RET NZ	POP BC	JP NZ nn	JP nn	CALL NZ nn	PUSH BC	ADD A, n	RST O	RET Z	RET	JP Z nn		CALL Z nn	CALL nn	ADC A, n	RST B
D	RET NC	POP DE	JP NC nn	OUT port, A	CALL NC nn	PUSH DE	SUB n	RST 16	RET C	EXX	JPC nn	IN A, Port	CALL C nn		SBC A, n	RST 24
E	RET PO	POP HL	JP PO nn	EX (SP), HL	CALL PO nn	PUSH HL	AND n	RST 32	RET PE	JP (HL)	JP PE nn	EX DE, HL	CALL PE, nn		XOR n	RST 40
F	RET P	POP AF	JP P NN	DI	CALL P NN	PUSH AF	OR N	RST 48	RET M	LD SP, HL	JP M nn	EI	CALL M nn		CP n	RST 56

Running machine code programs on the ZX81

To execute a machine code program on the ZX81, a section of memory in the RAM must be reserved so that the list of two-digit hexadecimal codes representing each instruction can be stored. The simplest method is to place a REM statement containing at least 50 characters at the start of the program file. Each character in the REM statement will occupy 1 byte in the memory. Starting at the byte used by the first character in the REM statement, each instruction code can be POKEd into the consecutive bytes.

A section of memory in the variable file can be reserved for a machine code program by creating either a long string or a large array. However, this has the disadvantage that it is liable to be moved about in the RAM and the addresses of the bytes where the instructions are stored will be altered.

The following program allows each instruction of a machine code program to be entered in turn and then POKEs it into the correct byte in the memory occupied by the characters in the REM statement.

Program 24—Machine Code Programmer

```
 1 REM .......... (50 full stops) ..........
10 FOR I = 16514 TO 16553
15 INPUT A$
20 IF LEN A$ <>2 THEN GOTO 15
25 POKE I, CODE A$(1) * 16 + CODE A$(2) - 476
30 PRINT A$; "□□";
35 IF A$ = "C9" THEN STOP
40 NEXT I
```

The FOR loop increments I from 16514, the address of the first character in the REM statement, to 16553, the address of the last character in the REM statement. The instruction is converted from hexadecimal to decimal by (CODE A$(1) – 28) * 16 + (CODE A$(2) – 28) and this can be simplified as in line 25.

When the instruction C9 is entered, the program will stop once the code has been POKEd into the correct byte. This is because C9 is the code for RETURN which signals the end of the machine code program.

All instructions must be entered as two digits; for example, 0A must be entered and not just A.

If a program requires more than 50 bytes, extra characters must be added to the REM statement and the terminating value of the FOR loop in line 10 must be modified.

The instruction 76h (HALT) should be avoided as the ZX81 would recognize this as the end of the REM statement. This is because 76h is the character CODE of NEWLINE.

We also need a program that allows an address to be specified and then displays all the instructions from that address onwards.

Program 25—Machine Code Display

```
 50 PRINT "INPUT STARTING ADDRESS"
 55 INPUT A
 60 CLS
 65 FOR I = 1 TO 20
 70 LET C = PEEK A
 75 LET D1 = INT (C/16)
 80 LET D2 = C - D1 * 16
 85 PRINT A; ".."; CHR$(D1 + 28); CHR$(D2 + 28)
 90 LET A = A + 1
 95 NEXT I
100 PAUSE 400000
105 GOTO 60
```

This program requires the starting address to be entered and then displays the machine code instructions in groups of twenty. Pressing BREAK will cause the program to stop. Pressing any other key will cause the next group of twenty codes to be displayed.

The function which executes a machine code program on the ZX81 is

USR n [F] 

This returns the contents of the register pair BC after running a machine code program from address n. Consider the following program stored in a REM statement by using Program 24.

Address	Instruction/Data (hex)	Mnemonic
16514	01	LD BC, nm (m =25) (n =30)
16515	25	
16516	30	
16517	C9	RETURN

If the following was executed

```
200 PRINT USR 16514
```

a value of 12325 (3025h) would be displayed.

RAMTOP

There is one other useful place for putting machine code programs. Referring back to Figure 11.2, there is a system variable called RAMTOP, address 16388/9, which points to the first address after the last existing byte in the RAM. This obviously changes, depending on how much memory is connected.

When NEW is executed, the RAM is cleared from the end of the system variables section up to the address before that contained in RAMTOP. By POKEing an address within the RAM into RAMTOP it is possible to reserve a section of RAM that is uneffected by NEW. A machine code program could be POKEd into the bytes in this reserved section.

Consider a standard 1K RAM ZX81 without any memory expansion. RAMTOP will be initially set to the value 17408. If 50 bytes were required for a machine code program 17358 should be POKEd into RAMTOP. The ZX81 is now 'fooled" into thinking the available RAM consists of the addresses from 16384 to 17357. However addresses 17358 to 17407 still exist and can be used to store the instructions of a machine code program.

One can practice using the different codes; although machine code programs are faster and more efficient with memory space than a high-level language, the drawbacks of them include that they are difficult to understand, program and read for errors, and the overall process is tedious.

STORING INFORMATION IN REM STATEMENTS

Information can be stored in a REM statement and obtained by PEEKing the corresponding address in the program file. For example, consider the problem of translating a sentence into Morse code. We need an efficient method of storing how each letter is represented in Morse code.

FIGURE 12.7

	CODE		CODE
A	•—	N	—•
B	—•••	O	———
C	—•—•	P	•——•
D	—••	Q	——•—
E	•	R	•—•
F	••—•	S	•••
G	——•	T	—
H	••••	U	••—
I	••	V	•••—
J	•———	W	•——
K	—•—	X	—••—
L	•—••	Y	—•——
M	——	Z	——••

One method is by using the diagram in Figure 12.8 which is called a *tree*; this consists of nodes with numbers which are connected by edges.

FIGURE 12.8

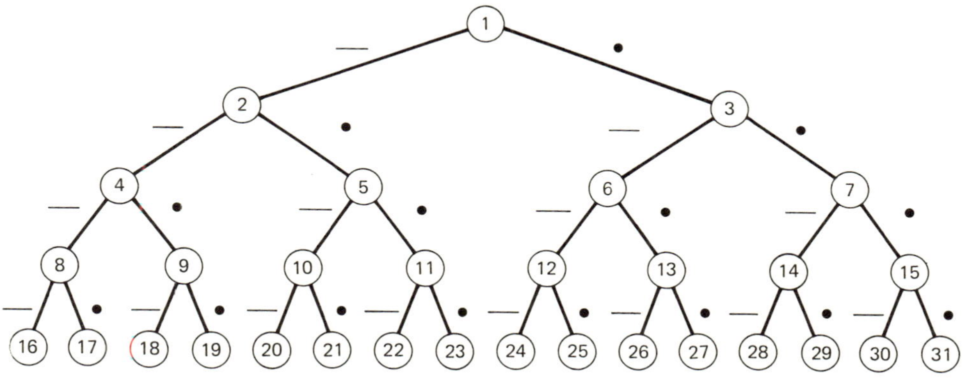

To find a number to represent a certain letter in Morse code, start at the top node in the tree with the number 1 in it. If the last symbol in the code is —, then travel down the left edge or if the last symbol is a •, then travel down the right edge:

J • — — —	travel left
B — • • •	travel right

From the new node, travel either left or right again depending on the second from last symbol in the code. Continue until all the symbols in the code have been used. The number arrived at represents the code for that particular letter:

B — • • • travel right, right, right, left.

The number which represents B is 30 and this is obviously a lot easier to store than — • • •. We now need a method of converting the number into the code.

The computer can translate 30 back into — • • • by the following:

i.	30	Even	PRINT "—"	1st symbol
ii.	INT (30 / 2) = 15	Odd	PRINT "•"	2nd symbol
iii.	INT (15 / 2) = 7	Odd	PRINT "•"	3nd symbol
iv.	INT (7 / 2) = 3	Odd	PRINT "•"	4nd symbol
v.	INT (3 / 2) = 1	STOP		

Continue dividing by 2 until the number becomes 1 and then STOP. If a number is odd, then PRINT "•", if it is even, PRINT "—".

We have now obtained a number representing the Morse code for each letter in the alphabet. These numbers will be stored in the bytes in the memory occupied by the characters in a REM statement. The addresses for each character are known to be as shown below if the REM statement is the first statement in the program file.

```
        a b c d e f g h i j k l m n o p q r s t u v w x y z
5 REM   * * * * * * * * * * * * * * * * * * * * * * * * * *

        address         address         address
        16514            16526           16539
```

For example, the number which represents the letter M will be stored at address 16526.

The value of the number which represents the Morse code form of each letter is obtained by PEEKing the relevant address in the range of 16514 to 16539.

The number representing each letter is in the range of 2 to 31. By adding 30 to each number, we obtain numbers in the range of 32 to 61. This enables the characters to be stored in the REM statement to be alphanumeric characters which are a lot neater and less error prone than graphic symbols. The REM statement will be

```
5 REM 7WSG5TEX9JCV68ARMFH4DPBOKU
```

The letter B, which is represented by the second character in the REM statement, is obtained by PEEKing address 16515. A value 60 would be PEEKed and if 30 is subtracted the value 30 is reached. We found earlier that 30 can be used to obtain the correct Morse code.

Program 26—Morse Code

```
 5 REM 7WSG5TEX9JCV68ARMFH4DPBOKU
10 CLS
15 INPUT A$
20 PRINT A$
25 FOR I = 1 TO LEN A$
30 LET C = CODE A$(I)
35 IF C = 0 THEN GOTO 75
40 LET A = PEEK (C + 16476) - 30
45 FOR J = 1 TO 4
50 IF A = 1 THEN GOTO 75
55 IF INT (A/2) * 2 = A THEN PRINT "—";
60 IF INT (A/2) * 2 < A THEN PRINT "•";
65 LET A = INT (A/2)
70 NEXT J
75 PRINT "/";
80 NEXT I
85 INPUT A$
90 IF A$ = "" THEN GOTO 10
```

To convert a sentence into Morse code, enter it as a string of characters followed by NEWLINE. Only alphabetic characters and spaces are allowed.

LINE RENUMBERING PROGRAM

By using the information from Figure 11.3, it is possible to write a program that will renumber a program listing in steps of 5. The object of this is to make a program appear neater when additional lines have been slotted in between others. The renumbering program will not change the GOTO and GOSUB statements numbers, so these must be corrected individually.

We situate the program from line 9990 so that it does not interfere with the main program.

Two variables are used, B and N. B is used to point at each address in the program file, that is, it starts at 16509 and is increased by 1 each time. N contains the number that will be used for the new line number. Every time it is used it is increased by 5 ready for the next line.

There are two tests in the program. The first is to check that the contents of addresses B and B + 1 are not 9990; if it is, then B is pointing to the address at the start of the line-renumbering program. Since these numbers are not required to be altered, the execution stops. The second test is to check for the NEWLINE character (see Figure 11.3). If one is found, it means the next two addresses contain the number of the next line and so N is POKEd into them.

Program 27—Line Renumbering

```
9990 STOP
9991 LET B = 16509
9992 LET N = 5
9993 POKE B, INT (N/256)
9994 POKE B + 1, N - 256 * INT(N/256)
9995 LET N = N + 5
9996 LET B = B + 1
9997 IF 256 * PEEK B + PEEK(B + 1) = 9990 THEN STOP
9998 IF PEEK (B - 1) = 118 THEN GOTO 9993
9999 GOTO 9996
```

Execute the program by RUN 9991 NEWLINE.

Since this program can be very time consuming with long program listings it is advisable to execute it in FAST mode.

USEFUL SYSTEM VARIABLES THAT CAN BE PEEKED AND POKED

16388/9	RAMTOP	The address of the first byte after the last byte in the RAM.
16396/7	D-FILE	Starting address of the display file.
16398/9	DF-CC	Address of the PRINT position in the display file.
16400/1	VARS	Starting address of the variable file.
16434/5	SEED	The seed for the random number generator.
16436/7	FRAMES	Television screen frame counter.

CHAPTER THIRTEEN

Loading and Saving

When power has been disconnected from the ZX81, the program and variables stored inside it are lost for good and so there is the facility for storing them on cassette tape so that they may be retrieved and used again later.

The ZX81 is connected to a cassette recorder by the twin wire cable with 3.5-mm jack plugs. Connect the microphone jack to the socket marked "MIC" on the ZX81 and the earphone jack to the socket marked "EAR."

SAVING A PROGRAM

To save a program on cassette tape do the following:

1. Cue up the part of the cassette tape which is to be used.
2. If required make a short voice recording containing the title of the program.
3. Type SAVE "name" [K] 

where name is the title of the program.
4. Start recording.
5. Press NEWLINE.

The screen will change first to grey then to black and white moving lines, and finally to the usual white.

The grey screen indicates that nothing is being recorded. The silent lead-in is to let the computer know, when loading, that a program is due. The moving black and white lines are the signal that the program is being recorded.

The program and its variables are now stored on the cassette tape.

LOADING A PROGRAM

To load a program from cassette tape do the following instructions:

1. Cue up the part of the cassette tape where the voice introduces the program.
2. Set the volume of the cassette recorder to three-quarters maximum, the treble, if available, to maximum, and the bass to minimum.
3. Type LOAD "name" [K] [LOAD J VAL] where name is the title of the program.
4. Start the tape.
5. Press NEWLINE.

After a short time the program will be loaded with its variables into the ZX81 memory. If there are any problems and the program does not seem to have been accepted then press NEWLINE.

If "name" is the empty string "", the ZX81 will load the first program it comes across on the tape.

SAVING AND LOADING PROBLEMS

To avoid any problems when saving and loading, these cautions should be taken:

1. Always make sure that the cassette recorder tape heads are clean. When cassette tape passes over the tape heads it leaves a small deposit. After a time this has mounted up until it becomes enough to muffle the recording to such an extent that the ZX81 is unable to decipher the signal.
2. Use high-quality tapes. Some poor quality tapes will not return a signal with a large enough voltage for the ZX81 to pick it up. If the signal is too low then the ZX81 will wait indefinitely for the program.
3. On a few cassette recorders it is important when loading that the MIC lead be disconnected. If this is not done, interference appears on the silent lead-in before the program, and the program cannot be loaded.
4. A few cassette recorders using mains voltage give interference as in (3), and if possible should be used with batteries.

5. The cassette recorder should be kept well away from the television because the recorder could pick up signals from the television, and these would be recorded on the program.
6. The volume should be set loud enough for the ZX81 to pick up the program, but not so loud that the program is distorted, or that interference is picked up on the silent lead-in.
7. The output of a stereo amplifier may damage a ZX81.

CHAPTER FOURTEEN

Crashing

When a program being executed fails either because of invalid data or because the program contains an error, it is said to have crashed. When control comes across an error, execution stops and an error code with the line number of the last line executed is displayed in the bottom left-hand corner. Usually if there are any errors in a program, they can be traced by knowing what the different error codes signify.

ZX81 ERROR CODES

- 0 Successful completion of program—no errors.
- 1 NEXT executed but corresponding control variable does not exist.
- 2 Undefined variable.
- 3 Subscript out of range.
- 4 Memory full.
- 5 Display file full.
- 6 Arithmetic overflow.
- 7 RETURN executed though no GOSUB exists.
- 8 INPUT used as a command.
- 9 Execution ceased due to STOP statement.
- A Invalid argument to function.
- B Integer out of range.
- C String does not contain an algebraic expression.
- D Program stopped by entering STOP at an INPUT statement or by pressing BREAK.
- E Unused.
- F Title of program when SAVEing is the empty string "".

If the error is still not obvious, the easiest method of tracing the fault is to include extra PRINT statements so that one can see the value of variables at intermediate stages in the program, and also what path the control takes.

USING STATEMENTS IN COMMAND MODE

It is possible to execute some of the ZX81 statements in command mode without putting the statement into a program. This is accomplished by typing the statement without a line number, for example,

```
PRINT 2.56 * 1.15  (NEWLINE)
```

first causes the screen to clear, then the result of the algebraic expression, 2.944, is displayed in the top left-hand corner of the screen, and finally the error code 0/0 is displayed in the bottom left-hand corner of the screen.

```
GOTO 200  (NEWLINE)
```

executes a program in the program file from line 200 without clearing the variables, as would happen if RUN 200 was used.

One of the best uses of this practice is for finding errors in a program. After a program has ceased execution, the values of selected variables can be obtained by the PRINT statement. The values stored in certain addresses can be obtained by using the PEEK function and the PRINT statement.

Additional STOP statements can be temporarily added to the program and the foregoing ideas used to find the intermediate values of variables. The program can be continued by executing CONT.

VALIDITY OF DATA

One method of preventing programs from crashing is to check that the data being entered are of the correct form. If the data are not correct then jump back to the same INPUT statement. The program should only continue if data of the correct form are entered.

```
INPUT data
IF (data not of correct form) THEN GOTO ( INPUT
                                          statement)
continuation of program
```

We shall now study a few examples of checking the different types of data being entered.

Alphabetical letters can be tested by checking their character codes. Sometimes the program requires an answer of either YES or NO. However typing either "Y" or "N" is quicker and so if the same question is to be answered several times it makes good sense to allow both forms to be accepted. This is achieved by checking the CODE of the first character of the input string.

```
100 PRINT "DO YOU WISH TO TRY AGAIN?"
105 INPUT Q$
110 REM CHECK FOR Y
115 IF CODE Q$ = 62 THEN GOTO 10
120 REM CHECK FOR N
125 IF CODE Q$ = 51 THEN STOP
130 GOTO 105
```

In fact any string entered beginning with Y is recognized as "YES" and any string beginning with N is recognized as "NO."

Numerical data can be verified to be within a certain range. To check a number is in the range of 1 to 5,

```
100 PRINT "ENTER THRUST"
105 INPUT T
110 REM CHECK T IS IN RANGE 1 TO 5
115 IF T < 1 OR T > 5 THEN GOTO 105
120 (continuation of program)
```

A hexadecimal number may be input as a string and converted to a numerical value by finding the CODE of each digit. The hexadecimal number can be checked to consist of only the digits 0, 1, ... F by ensuring the CODE of each digit is in the range of $28 <= x <= 43$.

```
100 INPUT A$
105 FOR I = 1 TO LEN A$
110 IF CODE A$ (I) < 28 OR CODE A$ (I) > 43
                              THEN GOTO 100
115 NEXT I
120 (continuation of program)
```

We can easily check string length with the LEN function. To check that a string has exactly 15 characters:

```
100 INPUT A$
105 IF LEN A$ <> 15 THEN GOTO 100
110 (continuation of program)
```

Always try to verify input data with an IF statement, unless memory is unavailable, since this makes programs very robust.

A useful technique is to input numerical data as a string and then to convert it to a numerical value. To input a positive number:

```
100 INPUT N$
105 LET N = VAL N$
110 IF N <= 0 THEN GOTO 100
```

Note that, in contrast to the majority of computers available, the ZX81 will show an error if the string argument of the VAL function does not contain a valid algebraic expression.

CHAPTER FIFTEEN

Programs and Programming Techniques

There is no better way to learn computing than to follow and try to understand another author's program. This chapter lists programs and explains how they function. Before trying to understand them, type the program into your ZX81 and execute it to see what actually happens. But first of all, here are some useful programming techniques.

CONSERVING MEMORY

A major problem with the basic ZX81 is its lack of memory available for the user. A full display uses well over 600 bytes, and this does not leave much memory space for the program file. This often means that an effective screen design is not possible. With 1K of memory you must learn to program efficiently and to use as little memory as possible.

The following methods reduce the amount of memory used.

1. Keep variable names as concise as possible. Every letter in a variable name uses one byte of memory, so if the name is mentioned several times a lot of memory is used unnecessarily.

2. Try to avoid REM statements. Although these statements are not executed by the computer, they still occupy valuable memory space.

3. Do not introduce unnecessary variables. For example, if a control variable I already exists but has finished its use, do not introduce a new control variable J; use I again. Every control variable uses 18 bytes, and so if J had been used, 18 bytes of memory space would have been wasted.

4. Never say in two lines what can be said in one.

```
10  LET A= PEEK 16396 + 256 * PEEK 16397 + 50
15  POKE A, 23
```

could be replaced by

```
10  POKE PEEK 16396 + 256 * PEEK 16397 + 50, 23
```

This saves the memory that variable A would occupy, and the memory required to store the extra program line.

5. As mentioned, the display file uses a large quantity of memory. From Figure 11.4 we saw how the display file fills up each line on the screen from the left-hand side and that spaces on the right-hand side of the screen are not held in the display file. So to reduce the amount of memory required, keep the information displayed to the left-hand side of the screen whenever possible.

6. Brackets are not required around the argument of a function if the argument consists of a single item.

i. SQR 64
This calculates the square root of 64. The result is 8.

ii. SQR 64 + 36
This calculates the square root of 64 and adds the result to 36. The result is 44.

iii. SQR (64 + 36)
This calculates the square root of the sum of 64 and 36. The result is 10.

7. Numerical constants contained in a program listing occupy one byte for every digit including the decimal point, plus an extra six. These following six bytes contain a CODE 126 in the first byte and the number stored in the next five bytes, in the form shown in Figure 11.5.

1	would occupy	7 bytes.
2.0	would occupy	9 bytes.
1.37563	would occupy	13 bytes.

These additional six bytes are not actually displayed in the program listing.

If a numerical constant is featured several times, many bytes are consumed superfluously. An efficient method is to assign the constant to a variable, and then use that variable in its place.

With a 16K memory expansion interfaced to your ZX81, memory becomes plentiful, and these ideas of efficiency need not be kept to. Programs can now be made clearer by using REM statements and variable names the meanings of which are obvious to the user, for example, MAX, TOTAL, SCORE, and so on. However, programs that are spread out take longer to execute.

Other ideas that should be incorporated in a program are:

1. Line numbers should go up in steps of 5 or 10 and certainly not steps of 1. If steps of 1 are used it is not possible to ammend and improve the program by entering additional lines between those already in the program.

2. Try to avoid using unnecessary GOTO statements, as this keeps the program flow neater and easier to follow or trace for any errors.

3. If memory space allows, check all input data as explained in Chapter 14.

4. Be careful of using INKEY$ near the start of a program. This is because to execute the program, RUN NEWLINE is typed. If a finger is left on the NEWLINE key for a split second, it may be picked up by INKEY$ and interfere with what was intended.

5. For short programs that will be required to be executed several times, include a GOTO statement at the bottom of the program so control will jump back to the start of the program. This saves the user from having to use RUN over and over. There should also be the opportunity for the user to return to command mode if he does not want the program to be executed again. A good method of handling these requirements is to use an INPUT statement requesting a string to be entered. If this string is the empty string "", then control returns to the start of the program. If any characters are entered then the execution of the program STOPs:

```
(program)
INPUT Q$
IF Q$ = "" THEN GOTO (top of program)
STOP
```

To return to the top of the program the user types the single key stroke of NEWLINE.

CONVERTING FROM OTHER DIALECTS OF BASIC

There are a number of statements available on some BASICs that are absent on the ZX81. The most important ones, and methods given for obtaining the same effect using alternative ZX81 BASIC statements, are listed.

1. The first few alternatives are to a number of string functions which return a substring from a specified string.

   i. LEFT$ (A$, N) This returns the first N characters starting at the first character from the string A$. This can be achieved with ZX81 BASIC by either A$ (1 TO N) or A$ (TO N).
   ii. RIGHT$ (A$, N) This returns the last N characters from the string A$. This can be achieved with ZX81 BASIC by either A$(LEN A$ – N + 1 TO) or A$(LEN A$ – N + 1 TO LEN A$).
   iii. MID$ (A$, M, N) This returns the first N characters starting at the Mth character from the string A$. This can be achieved with ZX81 BASIC by A$ (M TO M + N – 1).
   iv. TL$ (A$) This returns the string A$ minus its first character. This can be achieved with ZX81 BASIC by either A$(2 TO LEN A$) or A$ (2 TO).

2. The ON—GOTO statement. This statement takes the form:

ON (algebraic expression) GOTO N1, N2, . . . ,Nm

where N1 to NM are a list of line numbers.

The algebraic expression is evaluated and control continues at the line number whose position in the list is the integer component of the algebraic expression.

```
20  ON X GOTO 50, 60, 70
```

If X = 1 then control continues at line 50
If X = 2 then control continues at line 60
If X = 3 then control continues at line 70
If X < 1 or X > 3 depends on the computer.

The same result can be obtained on a ZX81 by using

GOTO (algebraic expression)

Consider the case above

```
20  GOTO 40 + X* 10
```

In some cases there is not an algebraic expression that gives the required line numbers and so logical operators have to be used, as explained in Chapter 9. Consider the same case again

```
20  GOTO (50 AND X = 1) + (60 AND X=2)
                        + (70 AND X=3)
```

3. The DATA, READ, and RESTORE statements. The DATA and READ statements are used for assigning large quantities of either numerical or string data to variables. This is most useful for assigning values to an array.

```
10  DATA 1, 2, 6, 24, 120, 720, 5040
```

To assign the values to the variables the READ statement is used.

```
15  DIM F(7)
20  FOR J = 1 TO 7
25  READ F(J)
30  NEXT J
```

If RESTORE is executed, the next item to be READ will be the first DATA item again.

This could obviously be achieved on the ZX81 by using several LET statements, but with a large quantity of data this would be very inefficient.

One satisfactory method would be to store the information in a string. The data can be retrieved by taking a substring:

```
10  LET A$="0001000200060024012007205040"
15  DIM F(7)
20  FOR J=1 TO 7
25  LET F(J)= VAL A$(4*J-3 TO 4*J)
30  NEXT J
```

Techniques such as these enable you to use programs published in magazines and books.

EXAMPLE PROGRAMS

Program 28—One-Armed Bandit

```
 5  RAND
10  LET S=500
15  LET A$="□ZX81□SILVERCHERRYORANGECAS
                         TLEKNIGHT□GOLD□"
20  FOR J=0 TO 21
25  PRINT AT 10,J; "■"
30  PRINT AT 11,J; "■"
35  PRINT AT 12,J; "■"
40  NEXT J
45  LET S=S- 5
50  PRINT S; "□□"
55  DIM B$(3,6)
60  FOR J=1 TO 3
65  LET B$(J)=A$(1 + 6* INT(RND*7) TO 42)
70  PRINT AT 11, 7*J- 6; B$(J)
75  NEXT J
80  LET S= S+ (10 AND B$(1)= B$(2))
          + (10 AND B$(1)= B$(3))
          + (10 AND B$(2)= B$(3))
85  PAUSE 300
90  GOTO 20
```

This program simulates a one-armed bandit or fruit machine. There are three barrels each having seven different types of symbols printed on it. They are then spun around and allowed to come to rest. One symbol on each barrel will then be seen through a window. Ten cents will be awarded if the same symbol is displayed in two of the windows and 30 cents will be awarded if a symbol is displayed in all three windows. The cost of one play is 5 cents. The player is initially given 500 cents, so 495 is the first value displayed. To stop the program press BREAK. For another play, press any key except BREAK or wait 5 seconds.

Variables:

A$	Contains seven sets of six characters, each set being a symbol on the barrels of the one-armed bandit.
B$(3,6)	Contains the three symbols seen through the windows.
S	Players credit.
J	Control variable.

line 5	Sets the sequence of random numbers to commence in an unknown position.
line 10	Sets player's initial credit to 500.
line 15	Assigns the characters of the names of the seven symbols on the barrels to string variable A$
line 20–40	Draws one-armed bandit onto the screen.
line 45	Deducts the cost of one play from the player's credit.
line 50	Prints player's credit onto the screen.
line 55	Reserves cells in memory for array B$(3,6)
line 60–75	Picks a symbol at random and assigns it to B$(J). This symbol is then printed onto the screen.

A$=

```
"□ZX81□SILVERCHERRYORANGECASTLEKNIGHT□GOLD□"
 ↑     ↑     ↑     ↑     ↑     ↑     ↑
 1     7     13    19    25    31    37
```

position of symbols

The position of each symbol is shown above. A random symbol is obtained by assigning the first six characters from position 1 + 6* INT(RND* 7)

line 80	Calculates how much money was won and adds it to the player's credit.
line 85	PAUSE for five seconds.
line 90	Jump to line 20 for next play.

Program 29—Patience

```
 5  RAND
10  CLS
15  LET A$="999999999"
20  LET A=28
25  LET M = 0
30  LET R = INT(1 + RND*RND*9)
35  PRINT AT 10,8;A$; AT 12,12; R
40  IF A$="000000000" OR A < 28 THEN GOTO 80
45  LET M = M + 1
50  LET P = CODE INKEY$ - 28
55  IF P < 0 OR P > 9 THEN GOTO 50
60  IF P = 0 THEN GOTO 30
65  LET A = CODE A$(P) - R
70  LET A$(P) = (CHR$ A AND A >=28)
                          +("*" AND A < 28)
75  GOTO 30
80  PRINT AT 18,0; "NUMBER OF MOVES ";M;
          AT 20,0; "PRESS NEWLINE TO PLAY
                                     AGAIN"
85  INPUT Q$
90  IF Q$ = "" THEN GOTO 10
```

Your task is to convert a string of nines to a string of zeros in the least number of moves. A random integer between 1 and 9 is displayed and this may be subtracted from one of the digits in the string provided the result is not less than 0. To subtract the number from the first digit, press 1, from the second digit, press 2, and so on up to the last digit, press 9. To pass press 0. When a string of zeros is obtained, the number of moves is displayed. For another game press NEWLINE while to return to command mode press any character followed by NEWLINE.
Variables:

A$	String of digits.
A	Code of digits changed.
M	Number of moves.
P	Position of digit changed.
R	Random integer.
Q$	Variable used for INPUT statement to halt program.

line 5	RAND causes the sequence of random numbers to commence in an unknown position.
line 10	Clear screen.
line 15	Set A$ to initial position.
line 20	Set A to 28.
line 25	Set M to 0.
line 30	Obtain random integer between 1 and 9. The use of RND * RND gives a bias towards the lower numbers.
line 35	Print on screen the current state of A$ and the random integer.
line 40	Check if A$ is a string of noughts or if the last digit changed became a value less than 0. If so game stops and control goes to line 80.
line 45	Increment M, (the number of moves) by 1.
line 50	Test for key being pressed.
line 55	If key pressed is not key '0' to key '9' or no key is pressed then go to line 50.
line 60	If key pressed was key '0' the player has passed so go to line 30 for next random integer.
line 65	Assign code of digit in string at the position required minus the value of the random integer to variable A.
line 70	Change digit in string at the position required to the new character. If this character is not a digit then a star is used.
line 75	Jump back to line 30.
line 80	Print on the screen the number of moves taken.
line 85	Input string Q$.
line 90	If Q$ is the empty string then jump back to line 10 for another game. If Q$ contains any characters the program stops.

8K ROM ZX80 Modifications:

i. line 50 PAUSE 40000
ii. line 52 LET P = CODE INKEY$ –28

Program 30—Treasure Hunt

```
  5  RAND
 10  LET X1 = INT(RND*10)
 15  LET Y1 = INT(RND*10)
 20  FOR I = 1 TO 10
 25  PRINT 10 - I; "▨▨▨▨▨▨▨▨▨▨"
 30  NEXT I
 35  PRINT "□ABCDEFGHIJ"
 40  INPUT B$
 45  LET X = CODE B$(1) - 38
 50  LET Y = CODE B$(2) - 28
 55  LET D$ =("□NORTH" AND Y1 >Y)
            +("□SOUTH" AND Y1 <Y)
            +("□EAST" AND X1 > X)
            +("□WEST" AND X1 < X)
            +("□££££" AND (X1 = X AND Y1 = Y))
 60  PRINT AT 13,0; B$; D$; "□□□□□□"
 65  PRINT AT 9 - Y, X + 1; "*"
 70  IF D$(2) ="£" THEN GOTO 90
 75  INPUT B$
 80  PRINT AT 9 - Y, X + 1; "□"
 85  GOTO 45
 90  PAUSE 240
 95  CLS
100  GOTO 10
```

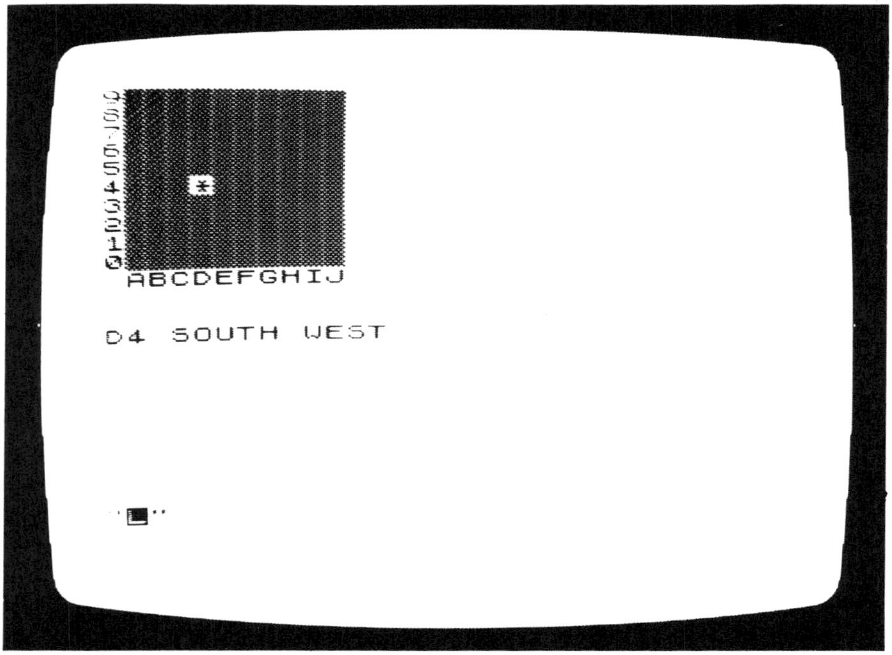

A casket of gold has been buried and your task is to recover it. A grid of 100 squares is drawn on the screen. Each square is labeled first by a letter corresponding to its column and second a number corresponding to its row. This label is called its coordinate. When entering a coordinate of a square, the computer will respond with the direction you must go to find the treasure. Continue until you find the treasure. After 4 seconds the game will restart automatically.
Variables:

X1	Column number where gold is hidden.
Y1	Row number where gold is hidden.
X	Column number of attempt by player.
Y	Row number of attempt by player.
B$	Coordinate of attempt by player.
D$	Direction player must proceed in to find gold.
I	Control variable.

line 5	RAND sets sequence of random numbers to commence in an unknown position.
line 10–15	Hide gold in a random position.
line 20–35	Draw grid on screen.
line 40	Input first attempt.
line 45–50	Convert coordinate into row number and column number by using CODE.
line 55	Calculate the direction the player must proceed in or if the gold has been found. The characters are assigned to string variable D$ if and only if the conditions after the ANDs are true.
line 60	Print out the result. Note that six blank spaces are printed after D$. This is because, for example, if NORTH is printed on top of SOUTH WEST, the screen displays NORTH WEST.
line 65	Draw a star at the position of the players attempt.
line 70	Check to see if the player has found the gold. If he has found the gold then goto line 90.
line 75	Input the players next attempt at the treasure.
line 80	Remove star of last attempt from the grid.
line 85	Jump back to line 45.
line 90	Gold found. Delay of 4 seconds before continuation of program.
line 95	Clear screen.
line 100	Jump back to line 10 to start again.

Program 31—Code Breaker

```
  5 RAND
 10 DIM A(4)
 15 DIM B(4)
 20 DIM C(4)
 25 FOR I = 1 TO 4
 30 LET B(I)=1 + INT (RND*6)
 35 NEXT I
 40 INPUT C$
 45 LET S = 0
 50 LET D = 0
 55 FOR I = 1 TO 4
 60 LET C(I) = CODE C$(I) - 28
 65 IF C(I) < 1 OR C(I) > 6 THEN GOTO 40
 70 LET A(I) = B(I)
 75 NEXT I
 80 FOR I = 1 TO 4
 85 IF A(I)<>C(I) THEN GOTO 105
 90 LET S = S + 1
 95 LET A(I) =-1
100 LET C(I) = 0
105 NEXT I
110 FOR I = 1 TO 4
115 FOR J = 1 TO 4
120 IF A(I)<>C(J) THEN GOTO 140
125 LET D = D + 1
130 LET A(I) =-1
135 LET C(J) = 0
140 NEXT J
145 NEXT I
150 PRINT C$;"-";S;D
155 IF S <> 4 THEN GOTO 40
```

Your task is to crack a four-digit code consisting of the numbers 1,2,3,4,5, and 6 by entering attempts and studying the clues returned. The clue will be of two digits. The first digit of the clue is the number of digits correct and in the correct position. The second digit of the clue is the number of digits correct but in the wrong position. The game stops when the correct code has been entered. Note that without the memory expansion the game is limited to 14 attempts (which should be plenty), as there is no more vacant memory for the display file to use.

Example Game	Attempt	Clue
	1234	20
	5656	01
	1225	20
	1266	10
	1353	12
	1153	22
	1135	40

Variables:

B(4)	Hidden code.
A(4)	Usually contains hidden code but may change when comparing with attempt.
C(4)	Code attempt.
C$	Code attempt digits held in string.
S	Number of correct digits in correct position.
D	Number of correct digits in wrong position.
I,J	Control variables.

line 5	Set sequence of random number to an unknown position.
line 10–20	Reserve cells in memory for arrays.
line 25–35	Assign a random hidden code to array B(4)
line 40	Input code attempt as a string of four characters.
line 45	Initialize S to zero.
line 50	Initialize D to zero.
line 55–75	For loop to do two things: (1) convert C$ to single digits and assign them to array C(4); (2) take hidden code in array B(4) and assign it to array A(4) ready to compare with array C(4).
line 80–105	Compare each digit in code with corresponding digit in code attempt. If they are different then continue with next digit. If they are the same increase S by 1. The two digits are then changed to 0 and –1. This is so they will not be considered again when comparing digits.
line 110–145	Compare each digit in code with all the digits in code attempt. If it comes across with two the same, then 0 is increased by 1 and the digits are changed to 0 and –1 so they will not be considered again.
line 150	Print out result.
line 155	If code has not been solved i.e. S <> 4. Then jump back for next go.

Program 32—Baccarat

```
  5  LET P = 50
 10  RAND
 15  LET T = 0
 20  PRINT "CREDIT "; P
 25  GOSUB 200
 30  GOSUB 200
 35  IF INKEY$ = "" THEN GOTO 35
 40  IF INKEY$ = "T" THEN GOSUB 200
 45  LET S = T
 50  PRINT "SCORE "; S
 55  PRINT
 60  PRINT "BANKER"
 65  LET T = 0
 70  GOSUB 200
 75  GOSUB 200
 80  IF T < S THEN GOSUB 200
 85  PRINT "SCORE "; T
 90  LET P = P - 1
 95  IF S > T THEN LET P = P + 2
100  IF INKEY$="" THEN GOTO 100
105  CLS
110  GOTO 15
200  LET C = INT (RND*13 + 1)
205  PRINT "A23456789TJQK"(C)
210  IF C > 10 THEN LET C = 10
215  LET T = T + C
220  LET T = T - 10*INT(T/10)
225  RETURN
```

This card game is played by you with the computer as the banker. The court cards are valued as 10 points, while the others are valued as their pip value. The object of the game is to obtain either two or three cards whose value is the nearest to nine when the multiples of 10 have been disregarded, for example, 12 counts as 2, 17 counts as 7, 24 counts as 4 and so on.

The computer deals two cards and you have two options:

i. 'Twist' a card press 'T'.
ii. 'Stick' press any other key.

The computer then tries to beat your score with either two or three cards. The banker wins one point if his score is greater than or equal to your score. You win one point if your score is greater than the banker's score.

For another play press any key.
Variables:

P	Credit
C	Card dealt.
S	Player's score.
T	Score used in subroutine and banker's score.

line 5	Set credit to 50.
line 10	Set sequence of random numbers to commence in an unknown position.
line 15	Set score to zero.
line 20	Print player's credit on the screen.
line 25–30	Call subroutine twice to deal two cards to the player.
line 35	Wait for a key to be pressed before continuation of program.
line 40	If key 'T' is pressed then deal another card by calling subroutine again.
line 45	Assign score to variable S.
line 50–60	Print score and "BANKER" on screen.
line 65	Reset T to zero.
line 70–75	Call subroutine twice to deal two cards to the banker.
line 80	If the banker's score is less than the player's score then call subroutine to deal the banker a third card.
line 85	Print banker's score on screen.
line 90–95	If banker has won, deduct one point from the player's credit, if not, add one point to the player's credit.
line 100	Wait for any key to be pressed before continuation of program.
line 105	Clear screen.
line 110	Jump back to line 15 for another play.

subroutine

line 200	Pick a random integer between 1 and 13.
line 205	Print on the screen the corresponding card dealt. This is done by taking a slice of the string "A23456789TJQK"
line 210	Court cards count as 10, so if a Jack, Queen, or a King is dealt then set C to 10.
line 215	Add value of card to total.
line 220	Deduct multiples of 10 from total.
line 225	Return to main program.

8K ROM ZX80 Modifications:

i. line 33 PAUSE 40000
ii. line 100 PAUSE 40000

Program 33—Eldorado

```
  5 DIM N(5)
 10 DIM V(5)
 15 FOR I = 1 TO 5
 20 LET V(I) = 300
 25 NEXT I
 30 LET C = 50000
 35 PRINT "AVIATION"
 40 PRINT "CHEMICALS"
 45 PRINT "ENERGY"
 50 PRINT "GOLD"
 55 PRINT "INSURANCE"
 60 FOR I = 1 TO 5
 65 PRINT AT I - 1, 10; V(I); "□□"; AT I-1, 15;
                        N(I); "□□";
 70 NEXT I
 75 PRINT C; "□□□□□"
 80 INPUT S$
 85 LET S = INT ((CODE S$ - 36)/2)
 90 LET N = VAL S$(2 TO )
 95 IF ABS N > 100 OR S < 1 OR S > 5 THEN GOTO 80
100 LET N(S) = N(S) + N
105 LET C = C - N*V(S)
110 FOR I = 1 TO 5
115 LET V(I) = V(I) + INT((RND - 0.5)* N)
120 IF V(I) < 5 THEN LET V(I) = 5
125 NEXT I
130 GOTO 60
```

Your task here is to make money by buying and selling shares in companies dealing with aviation, chemicals, energy, gold, and insurance. The screen displays how much one share of each company costs and they will be seen to fluctuate up or down. You initially have $50000, and this is displayed.

To buy shares in a company, enter a string containing first the initial of the company and then how many shares you wish to purchase.

To buy 25 shares in GOLD enter	"G25"
To buy 30 shares in ENERGY enter	"E30"

To sell shares in a company enter a string containing first the initial of the company and then the negative value of how many shares to be sold.

To sell 50 shares in CHEMICALS enter	"C–50"
To sell 60 shares in AVIATION enter	"A–60"

The buying and selling of shares is limited to a maximum of 100 shares at a time. To buy 200 gold shares must be done in two operations.

If your money goes negative (in debt), you must sell some shares immediately before you buy any more.

Variables:

N(5)	Array containing number of shares of each company held.
V(5)	Value of a single share for each company.
C	Credit—how much money you have.
S$	Used to input string telling computer of either purchase or sale of shares.
S	Numerical name of share to be either bought or sold.
N	Number of shares to be bought (positive) or sold (negative).
I	Control variable.

line 5	Set up array N(5).
line 10	Set up array V(5).
line 15–25	Set initial values of shares to 300.
line 30	Set initial credit of 50000.
line 35–55	Print out companies on screen.
line 60–70	Print out values of shares and how many are held on screen.
line 75	Print out credit. Note this is followed by a string of spaces so that any digits remaining from the credit before are removed.
line 80	Input S$ the string to tell the computer what you want to buy or sell.
line 85	Take first character and convert "A" to 1, "C" to 2, "E" to 3, "G" to 4 and "I" to 5. Assign value to S.
line 90	Take remaining characters and convert them into a numerical value and assign it to N.
line 95	Check that S lies between 1 and 5 inclusive and N is between 100 and –100 inclusive. If not, go back to line 80 and input S$ again.
line 100	Amend number of shares held.
line 105	Amend credit.
line 110–125	Share values allowed to fluctuate using RND. The share value of any company is not allowed to drop below 5.
line 130	Jump back to line 60 to print on the screen the amended values of the shares and give the player another option to purchase or sell shares.

Program 34—Prisoner's Dilemma

```
 5  RAND
10  LET T = 0
15  PRINT AT 4, 5; "PRISONERS DILEMMA"
20  PRINT AT 7, 5; "TOTAL SENTENCE "; T
25  PRINT AT 9, 2; "DO YOU WISH TO CONFESS? ";
30  LET A = (CODE INKEY$ - 51)/11
35  IF A <> 1 AND A <> 0 THEN GOTO 30
40  PRINT INKEY$
45  LET B = INT(RND*2)
50  IF B = 1 THEN PRINT AT 11, 2;
             "PRISONER 2 HAS CONFESSED"
55  IF B = 0 THEN PRINT AT 11, 0;
             "PRISONER 2 HAS NOT CONFESSED"
60  LET S = 2 + 8 * B + 4 * A * B -2* A
65  PRINT AT 13, 0; "YOU ARE SENTENCED TO ";
                    S;" YEARS"
70  LET T = T + S
75  INPUT Q$
80  CLS
85  IF Q$ ="" THEN GOTO 15
```

8K ROM ZX80 Modifications:

i. line 27 PAUSE 40000
ii. line 35 Alter the GOTO statement so that when executed control jumps to line 27

You are one of two prisoners being held separately in custody on the charge of producing forged bank notes. The officer in charge does not have sufficient evidence to convict the prisoners and so approaches each prisoner in turn. He will give the prisoners the opportunity to confess and give evidence against each other. In return he will let that particular prisoner go free, while the prisoner who does not confess will be given a sentence of 10 years in prison. If neither prisoner confesses, then they both will be sentenced to 2 years in prison, and if they both confess, they will be sentenced to 12 years in prison.

You and your fellow prisoner have both previously agreed to deny the charge and get 2 years imprisonment each. However, you have the dilemma that you cannot trust him and think he may confess, in which case he will go free and you will get 10 years.

RUN the program and when given the choice of confessing, touch either the key 'Y' to confess or key 'N' to deny the charge. The computer tells you how many years you have been sentenced to in prison. Press NEWLINE to play again, and any character followed by NEWLINE to return to command mode.

A	Your decision	1—Confession. 0—No confession.
B	Other prisoner's decision	1—Confession. 0—No confession.
S	Number of years sentence.	
T	Total years sentence.	

This program is very simple except for an efficient method of calculating the number of years sentenced.

line 5	RAND causes sequence of random numbers to commence in an unknown position.
line 10	Initialize T, total number of years sentenced to zero.
line 15	Print title on screen.
line 20	Print total number of years sentenced on screen.
line 25	Print option for player.
line 30–35	Tests for key 'N' or key 'Y'. If key 'N' is pressed assign 0 to A. If key 'Y' is pressed assign 1 to A.
line 40	Print either "Y" or "N".
line 45	Prisoner 2 makes his decision.
line 50–55	Print prisoner 2's decision on screen.
line 60	Calculate sentence for the player. This can be evaluated by the following four IF statements.

```
60  IF A = 1 AND B = 1 THEN LET S = 12
61  IF A = 1 AND B = 0 THEN LET S = 0
62  IF A = 0 AND B = 1 THEN LET S = 10
63  IF A = 0 AND B = 0 THEN LET S = 2
```

but this is inefficient with memory space.
The following is more efficient.

```
60  LET S = 12 AND (A = 1 AND B = 1) +
             0 AND (A = 1 AND B = 0) +
            10 AND (A = 0 AND B = 1) +
             2 AND (A = 0 AND B = 0)
```

However since A and B are either 0 or 1, it can be written:

```
60  LET S = 12 * A * B +
             0 * A * (1 − B) +
            10 * (1 − A) * B
             2 * (1 − A) * (1 − B)
```

Which can be simplified to

```
60 LET S = 2 + 4 * A * B + 8 * B − 2 * A
```

line 65 Print out sentence for player.
line 70 Calculate total number of years sentence for player.
line 75 INPUT statement, enter a string to stop.
line 80 Clear screen.
line 85 Test to see if an empty string "" was entered at line 75. If so, jump back to line 15.

Program 35—Destination Saturn

```
 5  PRINT AT 5, 6; "DESTINATION SATURN"
10  PRINT AT 10, 0;
    "HEIGHT □□□ VELOCITY □□ THRUST □□ FUEL"
15  LET S = 800
20  LET F = 800
25  LET V = 125
30  LET A = 0
35  IF INKEY$ = "" THEN GOTO 50
40  LET A = CODE INKEY$ − 33
45  IF ABS A > 4 THEN LET A = −4
50  LET F = F − 2*(4 + A)
55  IF F < 0 THEN LET F = 0
60  IF F = 0 THEN LET A =−4
65  LET S = S − V/4 − 2 * A
70  LET V = V − 2 * A
75  PRINT AT 12, 0; INT (S AND S > 0); "□□"; TAB 9;
                   V;"□□"; TAB 19; 5 + A; "□□";
                   TAB 27; F;"    "
80  IF S > 0 THEN GOTO 35
85  IF V > 10 THEN PRINT AT 15, 5;
                "▞▞▞▞▞□ CRASH □▚▚▚▚▚"
```

8K ROM ZX80 modification: Add line 77—PAUSE 150

You are the captain in charge of the space shuttle 'Columbia' and your mission is to land safely on the surface of the planet Saturn. Your on board computer is a ZX81. You initially have 800 units of fuel, the initial velocity is 100, and the height above the surface is 800. The shuttle's rockets are operated by touching keys 1 to 9 on the ZX81

1	2	3	4	5	6	7	8	9
↑				↑				↑
No thrust (acceleration −4)				Thrust equal to force of gravity. (acceleration 0)				Large thrust (acceleration +4)

To change thrust, touch the required key until the new thrust has been displayed on the screen. If no key is touched, then the thrust remains unaltered.

The larger the thrust from the shuttle's rockets, the more the rate of descent will be decreased. However, a large thrust uses up more fuel than a small thrust. When all the fuel has been used up, the shuttle will plunge to the surface by the force of gravity.

The shuttle will survive an impact on landing if the velocity is less than 10.

Variables:

S	Height of shuttle above surface of planet.
F	Fuel remaining in shuttle's fuel tanks.
V	Velocity of shuttle.
A	Acceleration of shuttle.

line 5–10	Print titles on screen.
line 15–30	Set variables to their initial values.
line 35	Check to see if there is any required change in rocket thrust.
line 40	Calculate the new acceleration of the shuttle using the character code of INKEY$.
line 45	Check the acceleration is valid.
line 50	Deduct quantity of fuel used which is proportional to the acceleration.
line 55–60	Check if fuel tank is empty. If it is empty, then set acceleration of shuttle to the acceleration due to gravity.
line 65	Calculate height above surface of planet.
line 70	Calculate velocity. The change in velocity is proportional to the acceleration.
line 75	Print shuttle's conditions on screen. Notice that after every result two blank spaces are printed. This ensures that no unwanted digits remain on the screen if the new number is shorter than the old.
line 80	Check if the shuttle has touchdown.
line 85	Check if the shuttle has survived.

To make the game harder, try reducing the initial quantity of fuel.

Program 36—Black Holes

```
 5  RAND
10  FOR I = 0 TO 31
15  PRINT AT 0, I; "█"
20  PRINT AT 7, I; "█"
25  PRINT AT I/5, 31; "██"
30  NEXT I
35  LET P = 35 + 256 * PEEK 16397 + PEEK 16396
40  POKE P + 194, 184
45  POKE P, 23
50  LET C = CODE INKEY$
55  IF C < 33 OR C > 36 THEN GOTO 50
60  LET D = (33 AND C = 34) - (1 AND C = 33)
          - (33 AND C = 35) + (1 AND C = 36)
65  POKE P, 0
70  LET P = P + D
75  IF PEEK P > 127 THEN STOP
80  POKE P, 23
85  IF RND > 0.5 THEN POKE P + D, 128
90  IF INKEY$ <>"" THEN GOTO 90
95  GOTO 50
```

8K ROM ZX80 modifications.

i. line 50 PAUSE 40000
ii. line 52 LET C = CODE INKEY$

You are again in charge of a space shuttle and your task is to reach a starship (inverse S) without being sucked into any black holes that may appear.

Your controls are keys 5, 6, 7, and 8, and their directions are the directions of the arrows printed on the key.

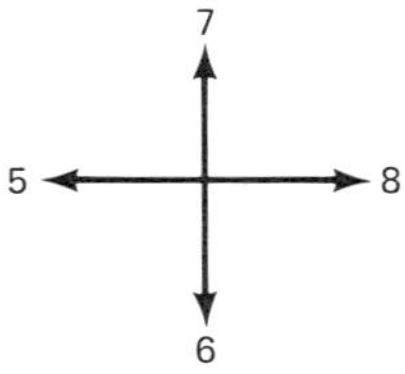

Variables:

P Position from top of display file where character is to be POKEd.
C CODE of character whose key is pressed.
D Direction of shuttle.

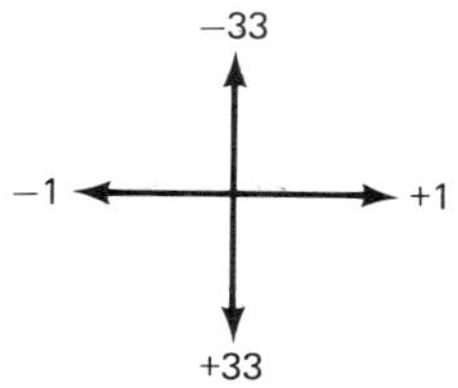

I Control variable.

line 5	RAND causes the sequence of random numbers to commence in an unknown position.
line 10–30	Set up display file.
line 35	Calculate starting address of display file and add 35, which is the address where the shuttle is initially positioned.
line 40	POKE starship onto screen.
line 45	POKE shuttle onto screen.
line 50	Calculate CODE of key being pressed.
line 55	Check key being presed is 5, 6, 7, or 8. If another key or no key is being pressed then control jumps back to line 50.
line 60	Calculate the number of places P has to be amended so that the shuttle can be POKEd into the new position.
line 65	POKE a blank space where the shuttle was before moving.
line 70	Amend P to the new address in the display file where the shuttle has moved to.
line 75	Check shuttle has not been sucked into a black hole or the shuttle has reached the starship. If it has, then game stops.
line 80	POKE shuttle into its new position in the display file.
line 85	A one-in-two chance that a black hole may appear in the position that the shuttle is moving.
line 90	Check finger has been taken off the keyboard. If this line was not there, the shuttle would be continually moving for as long as you had your finger on the key.
line 95	Jump back to line 50.

Program 37—Invaders

```
 5  LET S = 0
10  LET I = 15
15  PRINT AT 0, I;
20  IF PEEK(1 + PEEK 16398 + 256 * PEEK 16399) = 60
                                 THEN GOTO 90
25  PRINT "▜█▛"
30  IF INKEY$ <> "X" THEN GOTO 55
35  FOR J =-8 TO 8
40  PRINT AT 8 - ABS J, I + 1;
             ("T" AND J < 0) + ("□" AND J> = 0)
45  NEXT J
50  LET S = S - 10
55  IF INKEY$ = "N" AND I > 0 THEN LET I = I - 1
60  IF INKEY$ = "M" AND I < 29 THEN LET I = I + 1
65  PRINT AT 14, RND*31; "W"
70  SCROLL
75  SCROLL
80  LET S = S + 1
85  GOTO 15
90  PRINT S
```

This program will not run on an 8K ROM ZX80.

Your shuttle is now under attack from invaders and to survive, you must dodge them either by moving left or moving right. To move left press 'N' or to move right press 'M'. A point is awarded for every invader that passes by. If the shuttle is trapped you can fire a laser shot—press 'X'. This destroys all invaders in its path but this deducts 10 points from your score. If an invader hits the center of the shuttle, the game stops and your score is displayed.

Variables:

S Score.
I Position of shuttle on top line.
J Control variable.

line 5	Initialize S to 0.
line 10	Initialize I to 15.
line 15	Set up PRINT position for shuttle.
line 20	Check shuttle has not been hit by an invader. As mentioned in Chapter 12, the system variable DF-CC address 16398/9 contains the address in the display file of the PRINT position. By PEEKing the next address the computer can check if the center of the shuttle will be printed on top of an invader (CODE 60).
line 25	PRINT shuttle.
line 30	Check if laser has been fired. If not GOTO 55.
line 35–45	Laser has been fired. This will print eight "T"s in a vertical line coming from the center of the shuttle and then print blank spaces on top of the "T"s. Any invader in line will be printed on top of and lost for good. ("T" AND J < 0) + ("□" AND J > =0) will print a "T" if J is less than 0 and a space if J is greater than or equal to 0.
line 50	Deduct 10 points from score for using laser.
line 55	If key 'N' is being pressed and the shuttle is not on the left edge of the screen, then deduct one from the shuttle's position, I.
line 60	If key 'M' is being pressed and the shuttle is not on the right edge of the screen, then add one to the shuttle's position, I.
line 65	PRINT an invader on line 14 of the screen at a random position.
line 70–75	SCROLL the screen up two lines. This gives the effect of the invaders moving upward toward the shuttle.
line 80	Increment the score by 1.
line 85	Jump back to line 15.
line 90	PRINT score.

CHAPTER SIXTEEN

Projects for Readers

1. Write a program to draw a line of random length and then request an attempt to guess how long the line measures in millimeters. Since the lengths of the lines will differ depending on the size of the screen used, the program must allow an initial line of, say, 30 graphic symbols to be measured. The computer will then be able to gauge the length of lines using any number of graphic symbols.

Develop the program so that the length of 10 lines is asked; a grade is then given for how accurate the guesses were overall.

2. Write a program similar to (1), but this time draw a rectangle and then request the area in square centimeters. Again the program will have to allow the screen to be calibrated. Similarly, develop the program so that a grade is given for how accurate the guesses were overall.

3. Write a coordinate game program similar to program 30 (Treasure Hunt), but this time have the treasure hidden somewhere in a three-dimensional space. The computer should respond to an attempt at finding the treasure by giving a message consisting of up to three of the following: UP, DOWN, FORWARD, BACKWARD, LEFT, RIGHT, or TREASURE FOUND.

Let variables XX, YY, and ZZ store the three coordinates where the treasure is hidden. These should be set to some initial random integer value within a suitable range such as 0 to 99. Let variables X, Y, and Z store the player's attempt at finding the treasure.

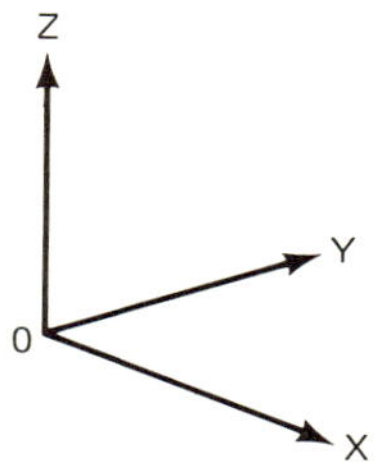

The computer should respond with either LEFT or RIGHT, depending on X and XX, either FORWARD or BACKWARD, depending on Y and YY, and either UP or DOWN, depending on Z and ZZ.

4. "The 3M + 1 Problem" An initial positive integer is chosen and then one of two operations is carried out on the number. Either

i. If the number if even, divide it by 2.
ii. If the number is odd, multiply it by 3 and add 1.

With the result repeat either (i) or (ii). This process should be continued until the number is 1.

The problem is that no number has yet been found that does not eventually reach 1, although mathematicians have been unable to prove that all positive integers should.

Write a program that allows a positive integer to be entered and assigned to a variable M. A check should be included to make certain that only positive integers are entered. Then the computer should keep processing either operation (i) or (ii) on M until it reaches 1. Display all intermediate results on the screen

Now try to find a number that does not reach 1!

5. Write a program that will draw different simple mazes. One method would be to draw several rectangles as shown in Figure 16.1.

FIGURE 16.1

and then to blank out certain sections of the inner horizontal lines at random, as shown, for example, in Figure 16.2.

FIGURE 16.2

Draw a symbol in the top left-hand corner of the maze to represent a fox. Allow the fox to be moved either up, down, left, or right by pressing certain keys, using the method of POKEing characters into the display file as explained in Chapter 12. Before the character is POKEd into the display file, the address should first be PEEKed to make sure the fox has not been moved onto a black square.

6. Develop project 5 to include a rabbit that moves randomly about the maze. The object now is for the rabbit to be caught by the fox.

7. If you have a 16K RAM Pack memory expansion, develop Program 37 (Invaders) so as to shoot down as many invaders as possible. Award a score for every invader demolished.

The method is to set up the PRINT position to print the "T" representing the laser by using PRINT AT. Then test to see if an invader is present by PEEKing the address containing the system variable DF-CC address 16398/9. Different types of invaders could be used, each worth different scores if eliminated.

8. Write a program to record the state of your financial position. An array could be created to hold the values of, for example, bank credit account, bank deposit account, national savings account, building society accounts, premium bonds, access credit card account, endowment insurances, stocks and shares, and so on. The program should allow the values to be modified when required. Remember that when the program is SAVEd, the contents of the arrays are also SAVEd. When the program is loaded, execute the program by using GOTO rather than RUN and then the arrays will not be cleared.

9. Write a program to keep a check on a record collection. A large two-dimensional array should be set up which could store, for each record, the title, the artist, and maybe to whom and when it was loaned. The program should allow for return of loaned records and new additions to the collection.

10. Write a program similar to that in Project 9, but this time to keep a check on programs for your ZX81 that are stored on cassette tape. The array should store the name of the program, the number of the cassette the program is stored on, where on the cassette the program can be found, and the quantity of memory required to run the program. The program should allow programs to be added or deleted from the list.

11. Write a program that stores French words and their English equivalents. Two arrays, F$(200,15) and E$(200,15), should be used where the French word is stored in F$(J), and the equivalent English word is stored in E$(J)—remember F$(J) is the same as F$(J, 1 TO 15). The alphabetical sorting routine, Program 4, can be used to keep the French words in alphabetical order.

The program should be used for translating French sentences into English. If a French word is used that is not in the known list, a subroutine should be called which requests the word to be looked up in a dictionary and the meaning entered. This word and its translation should then be added to the array so that if the word is asked again, the answer can be given.

12. Write a program that could be used by a business for a mailing list. If the printer is attached, the addresses could be printed onto paper and then stuck on the envelopes to be sent. The program should allow names and addresses to be either added or deleted from the list.

Use an array L$(100, 75) to store the information where L$(I) can store each name and address. Store the

name in	L$(I, 1 TO 15)
address in	L$(I, 16 TO 35)
town in	L$(I, 36 TO 55)
county in	L$(I, 56 TO 67)
post-code in	L$(I, 68 TO 75)

How would you print out only the addresses which are in, for example, Albany or Chicago?

13. Write a program using the timing facility described in Chapter 12 to time the length of telephone calls. The charge code should be entered and from the time the telephone call commences, the current cost of the call should be continually displayed on the screen.

Develop the program so a track is kept on all telephone calls since the last telephone bill.

14. Write a program to play zeros and crosses against the computer. Use a 3 × 3 array to store the board positions. Store a

1 if there is no piece positioned
2 to represent a 'X' (computer's piece)
3 to represent a 'O' (player's piece)

Write a section of program which uses the array to print a zeros and crosses board and the X's and the O's correctly positioned.

It is possible to tell what state each of the eight possible winning lines is in by multiplying the three values in the array representing the line together.

State	Values of Line
. . .	1*1*1=1
X . .	2*1*1=2
O . .	3*1*1=3
X O .	2*3*1=6
X X .	2*2*1=4
O O .	3*3*1=9
X X O	2*2*3=12
O O X	3*3*2=18
X X X	2*2*2=8
O O O	3*3*3=27

When the computer has to choose a position for its move, an ordered list of strategies is needed. If the computer cannot do strategy 1, then it tries strategy 2. If it cannot do strategy 2, then it tries strategy 3, and so on until it can do one of the strategies.

A suggested list of strategies is for the computer to place its piece in the first line that is:

1.	Value 4	Produce winning line for computer.
2.	Value 9	Block winning line for player.
3.	Value 3	Block a possible winning line for player.
4.	Value 2	Produce a possible winning line for computer.
5.	Value 1	Empty line, move into the center position.
6.	Value 6	Move into line containing one X and one O.

It is up to the programmer to order these strategies in a way that he feels will produce the strongest game.

15. Write a program to play a game of Nim against the computer.

The rules of the game are simple. A number of coins, matches, or something similar are divided into three piles. The two players take it in turn to remove one or more items from one of the piles. The player who takes the last item wins; a variation is whoever takes the last item loses.

It is possible to write a program that the computer removes enough items from one of the piles to leave the state of the game "safe," that is, provided it plays with the same strategy it cannot lose.

To find out if a position is safe, the number of items in each pile is written using binary notation. The numbers are written above each other. The state of the game is defined as safe if each column adds up either zero or an even number.

Consider three piles containing six, three, and seven items.

```
6   0110
3   0011
7   0111
    ----
    0232
```

The state would be safe by making the column adding up to 3 into a column adding up to 2 or 0, e.g. by taking two items from the first pile.

```
4   0100
3   0011
7   0111
    ----
    0222
```

16. Write a program to play a reasonable game of checkers.

The first problem is to find a way of storing the board positions. One simple way would be to use an 8 × 8 two-dimensional array where each element would store

−1	if the square was a square that a piece may not be moved on
0	if no piece is positioned
1	if a black piece is positioned
11	if a black king is positioned
2	if a white piece is positioned
22	if a white king is positioned

The starting positions will be:

8	−1	2	−1	2	−1	2	−1	2
7	2	−1	2	−1	2	−1	2	−1
6	−1	2	−1	2	−1	2	−1	2
5	0	−1	0	−1	0	−1	0	−1
4	−1	0	−1	0	−1	0	−1	0
3	1	−1	1	−1	1	−1	1	−1
2	−1	1	−1	1	−1	1	−1	1
1	1	−1	1	−1	1	−1	1	−1
	1	2	3	4	5	6	7	8

Write a section of program so that the contents of this array can print a checkers board with the pieces positioned correctly.

Write a section of program so that a player may specify a move and both the contents of the array storing the board positions and the screen are modified accordingly. The program should check that the move is legal.

The next stage is to devise some strategies for the computer's moves, for example:

1. If a move exists for the computer in which it can take a player's piece by jumping over it then this should be done. Remember it is legal for a piece to jump over more than one of the opponent's pieces.
2. Move pieces on as far as possible, without being taken, to make Kings.
3. Check that when a King moves it moves into a safe position so that it will not be taken.

Start off by writing about three strategies in your program and then gradually develop it by adding additional ideas until it becomes a reasonable player.

Anyone interested in game playing on computers should obtain a book specializing on the matter. One good one is *Game Playing with Computers* by D. D. Spencer, published by Hayden.

Glossary

Address
Position of location in memory.

Algorithm
Method of solving a specific problem.

BASIC
A simple high-level computer language.

Baud
Data signaling rate (bits per second).

Binary
Number representation system with a radix of two.

Bit
A single BInary and digiT.

Bug
Error in program causing malfunction.

Byte
A group of eight bits.

Carry
Digit being added to next column when a column exceeds the radix.

CPU
Part of the computer which processes the information and controls the other units.

Execute
Perform the sequence of instructions in a program.

Hardware
Physical components making up a computer system.

High-level language
A simple program language which has to be turned into machine code before it can be processed.

Interface
Physical unit which links two separate components in a computer system.

I/O
Input/output.

K
1024 or 2^{10}

Machine code
Low-level language which can be processed by the computer.

Peripheral
Physical component for the input or output of information.

Program
Sequence of instructions.

Radix
Base of a numbering system.

RAM
Memory in which data can be stored or obtained from any address.

ROM
Memory in which the contents were entered when manufactured and which cannot be altered.

Software
A computer program.

Volatile storage
Memory which loses its contents when the power is removed.

Word
Group of bits.

Index